The Irish Roots of Margaret Mitchell's *Gone With the Wind*

David O'Connell

Claves and Petry, Ltd.
P. O. Box 3075
Decatur, GA 30031
Phone/Fax (404) 370-1761

1996

Published by: Claves & Petry, Ltd.
               Post Office Box 3075
               Decatur, GA 30031

Margaret Mitchell's letter on pp. 16-17, 42, 91© 1996 by Suntrust Bank Atlanta, as executor under the will of Stephens Mitchell.

Library of Congress Catalog Card Number: 96-85469
ISBN 0-9653093-0-4

The text of this book is composed in Times New Roman.

To
Mary Rose Taylor
with admiration, affection and gratitude

Table of Contents

II The Catholic Roots

Acknowledgments

I am indebted to a number of people in writing this book. At the top of the list is Mary Rose Taylor, founder of Margaret Mitchell House, Inc. in Atlanta. It was she who had the initial vision to transform "The Dump," as Mitchell referred to the apartment house where she lived while writing *GWTW*, into a museum and cultural center. Despite many setbacks, including two fires, one in September 1994 and the other in May 1996, that almost killed the project, she pressed on. Now, on the eve of the opening of Margaret Mitchell House, the harvest of her effort has become visible in many ways. The most tangible one for me is the vast amount of new information that has come to light. Now that there is a living center for Margaret Mitchell studies, pictures, letters, lost manuscripts and other related items of interest have been discovered and made available to her. She in turn has shared many of these items with me. Without her support, the present essay could not have been written.

At Margaret Mitchell House, the Principal Researcher, Noëlle King, has also made available to me much of the fruit of her own personal research, including records from Immaculate Conception and Sacred Heart churches, newspaper and book sources, Stephens and Fitzgerald family pictures and recollections, and others related materials. She has also put me in touch with many other admirers of Margaret Mitchell's novel. To her I express once again my gratitude. At the Atlanta History Center, I would like to thank Tammy Gallaway and Michael Rose for their advice. Librarian Sara Saunders was also especially helpful to me, while Franklin Garrett, the eminent historian of Atlanta, came to my aid to confirm that Fitzgerald Street in Atlanta is in fact named after the Fitzgeralds in Margaret Mitchell's Irish and Catholic family tree. In tracking down the relationship between Sister Mary Melanie and Melanie Hamilton of *GWTW*, Victoria Wilcox of the Holliday House Association in Fayette County has been of invaluable help. At Georgia State University, archivist Peter Roberts was very helpful with pictures from the GSU collection, while Margie Patterson, of the Interlibrary Loan Department, helped me with this book just as she has done in the past with earlier efforts of mine. Also at Georgia State, Professors Elizabeth Stanfield and Harold Dickerson read the manuscript and offered many helpful suggestions, while Dolores Shelton, computer wizard extraordinary, help prepare the text for publication. My thanks also go to Professor Maxine Turner of Georgia Tech, to Betty Talmadge of Lovejoy Plantation, to Don O'Briant of the *Atlanta Journal-Constitution*, to historian Joseph Moore of Clayton County, and to Fr. Stephen T. Churchwell, pastor of Sacred Heart Parish in Atlanta, for their help.

The help and advice received have been most appreciated. However, I bear exclusive responsibility for the opinions and interpretations expressed in the pages that follow.

Introduction

When confronted by the wonder of *GWTW*, the most widely read novel in the history of world literature and the most widely sold book after the *Bible*, one is at a loss to explain it. How could a diminutive woman in her mid-20's, who had been a gifted but generally underachieving high school student and a college dropout, achieve such a creative miracle? Where did she derive the inspiration to write a novel of over a thousand pages, while at the same time keeping the reader enthralled from beginning to end? By what stroke of genius did she come up with a name like Scarlett O'Hara for her heroine? And what hidden resources did she draw upon to make this girl's experience so compelling and believable for millions of readers of diverse cultures around the world? In other words, by what miracle of creative genius does Scarlett, a daughter of an Irish immigrant, born into a rural area in an underdeveloped part of an agrarian state, attain universal recognition and validity? The answer to this question is not only very complex, it has also remained largely unasked by literary scholars. For these two reasons, no ready answer has been available until now.

In the present study, I make an effort to solve this puzzle. And I do so by delving into Margaret Mitchell's Irish and Catholic family roots. As the granddaughter and great granddaughter of Irish immigrants, Mitchell received intact a massive amount of oral lore about her mother's Irish Catholic pioneer family. Notwithstanding the important attributes that she owed to her father's forebears, which surface from time to time in the narrative of *GWTW*, it is in the legacy of the Irish-born Fitzgerald/Stephens side of her family that we find the seeds that would later blossom into *GWTW*.

The genetic inheritance of every human being is a miraculous combination of two seemingly infinite streams. They influence not only physical appearance and overall bodily health, but also personality and intelligence. In the case of Margaret Mitchell, her genetic inheritance was most complicated and, as usually happens in this regard, it is difficult to trace the many strands back to their various points of origin. Yet, with certain caveats in place, it is possible to do this in her case.

Mitchell's father's family were of solid stock. Georgians for several generations and Atlantans since the city had come into existence, they were hard working Methodists who served both God and society. They were also people of more than modest means who were respected in their communities. Among the debts that Mitchell owed to this family stream were, first of all, her looks. By all accounts, her facial features were those of a Mitchell. She also seems to have owed them her capacity for hard work and independence of mind (although her mother's family also possessed these attributes in abundance). To be sure, there were also eminent Civil War veterans on the Mitchell side of the family and these folk had also endured real hardships during that period of time. Finally, the Mitchells also delighted in story telling. But when it came time to write *GWTW*, it was the Fitzgerald/Stephens side of her family that provided the necessary spark of inspiration, because it was among these folk that she derived both the tragic view of life that undergirds *GWTW* and the overall scaffolding on which the narrative is built. In a word, it was the bardic element in Mitchell's mother's family that provided the impetus for this great work.

***

I trace her literary genius back to its origins in her childhood. In particular, I focus on the Irish and Catholic roots of her experience. The Fitzgerald/Stephens side of her family played a preeminent role in sparking her literary vocation. As a girl, she visited the former Fitzgerald plantation in Clayton County many times. Her Fitzgerald great aunts still lived there. The property, known as Rural Home, and the stories that went with it, were part and parcel of her being. Baptized and raised as a Catholic, she had an intimate knowledge of and appreciation for pre-Vatican II spirituality. She, like Scarlett, examined her conscience the way Catholic girls were trained to do in those days. She also had an appreciation for the beauty of the Latin rite with its prayers for every major occasion. She was sensitive, for instance, to the cult of the Blessed Virgin, which reached unprecedented levels of fervor and popularity during the first half of the 20th century. It is not for nothing that the phrase "Mother of God," and the formulaic prayer in her honor, known as the rosary, resonates from one end of *GWTW* to the other! She, like so many liberated young people, thought she had renounced her Catholic faith for good after her return from Smith College in Massachusetts in 1919. At this time she announced that she no longer considered herself to be a Catholic. Yet, ironically, her Catholic faith and her Irish heritage were not so easily thrown overboard. In fact, consciously or not, they wound up providing some of the essential ingredients of her novel. Without them, she could never have written the book that has become a cultural icon of worldwide significance.

I have been convinced, since my first complete reading of the novel in 1966, that what I call "the Irish element" in *GWTW* is terribly undervalued. I was in Georgia at the time, in the Infantry School at Fort Benning, waiting to go to Vietnam. I was struck by how Mitchell had her sense of place exactly right. The words on the page bring the people of Georgia and the state's climate, soil and vegetation to life. The sights and smells are all there. The book is as "real" as literary realism can be. But, I thought, isn't this what Southern writers have always been known for? Aren't they supposed to excel at creating a sense of place? So while I acknowledged her success here, I wasn't terribly surprised by it.

My big question lay elsewhere. Why, I wondered, did she give her heroine, who was to become the most famous character in American (and perhaps world) literature - an obviously Irish and Catholic name? As a native New Yorker, I had always been led to believe that Southern society was "homogeneous," while that of the North was "heterogeneous." According to the prevalent myth, everybody in the South was a WASP, and there were no "ethnic groups," unless of course one considered black folks to be ethnics. Some white Southerners were Baptists, some were Methodists, and some Presbyterians or Episcopalians, but in the end they were all WASPS. It was only in the North that you were supposed to find "ethnic groups." So a girl with a name like Scarlett O'Hara, whose mother led the family in reciting the rosary every evening, and whose father still spoke with a brogue, was someone you would expect to meet in a fictional work set in New York, Boston, Philadelphia or Chicago, but not in rural Georgia! I read the novel again the following year and pondered these questions anew. This second reading was slow, systematic, and detailed. Set against the background of war and destruction in which we, as GIs, were backing one party to a civil war, it convinced me that *GWTW* was truly a masterpiece.

***

GWTW is the closest thing we have in our culture to an *Odyssey* or an *Iliad*. Why? Because it sings of the greatness and weakness, the guiding myths and the harsh realities, the points of union and the horrible contradictions of our culture. It brings these issues to life at a time of great turmoil, the period of the Civil War and its aftermath. In foregrounding the experiences of Scarlett O'Hara and those close to her, Margaret Mitchell also paints a vivid picture of the age in which Scarlett lived. And that social context, although it has surely evolved since the days of the Civil War and Reconstruction, is still quite recognizable today. Indeed, some might be tempted to say that it is substantially the same: North vs. South, haves vs. have nots, black vs. white, immigrant vs. the established Americans, and so on.

GWTW is truly the most American work of fiction in our national literature. On one level it tells of Scarlett O'Hara and her quest for love, self-understanding and financial independence, but through her it is also the saga of the American people as a whole. For Scarlett, like most of us, is of modest social origins. Although she might appear at first sight to be wealthy - after all, her father owns land and slaves - he is also an immigrant without any formal education, and he speaks with a foreign accent. He is anything but a coastal aristocrat with access to those in power. In fact he is a very minor player in the overall social system - just as each of us is. And he is by no means assured that what he owns at the beginning of *GWTW* will still be his a few years down the road. Sound familiar? In a word, the novel brings to life the fragility, injustices and inconsistencies of our social system; and it does so by detailing the lives of ordinary Americans, not the gentry.

Another reason why I make the claim that *GWTW* is the closest thing we have to a national epic is because its success is based primarily on *word of mouth*. Millions upon millions of Americans have found out about the book in this way. Many readers, once they have encountered it, are hooked for life. Sadly, this process must take place in spite of the educational establishment. One can go through the entire sequence of courses leading to a college degree, even majoring in English, and never hear those four words mentioned! For reasons of political correctness, the work is not included on reading lists in high schools and colleges, and professionals on each of these levels tend not to even mention its name. This is a sad commentary on the degree to which so many members of the liberal educational establishment have abdicated their responsibilities. Instead of reading the book in an objective manner, too many of them dismiss it summarily with derogatory slogans.

In 1984, while teaching at the University of Illinois at Chicago, I had the opportunity to make yet another pilgrimage to Georgia, *GWTW* in hand. I read the novel once again. Then, four years later, I moved to Atlanta for good when I accepted a faculty position at Georgia State University. I was finally in a position to work seriously on this long-deferred project!

The present essay is part scholarly essay and part labor of love. It is intended not so much to convince the reader that *GWTW* is the epitome of American literary achievement, as to bring to light for those who already admire it certain aspects of the novel that have never been systematically elucidated. My reading does not pretend to negate the many other readings that are possible, some of which have already been done. It seeks rather to complement such efforts.

Now, more than ever, *GWTW* needs to be read and understood. The present work is a long-deferred contribution to that process.

Part I
The Irish Roots

Chapter 1:
The Irish Roots

What Does the Word "Irish" Mean in *GWTW?*

The word "Irish" is used throughout *GWTW*. No other nationality or ethnic group is specifically cited as often as this one. Perhaps the primary use of the word is to refer to the peasant origins of the O'Hara family. Thus, despite Scarlett's lack of formal education and social sophistication, she does have that special kind of "hard-headed Irish sense" (172) that we associate with peasants.[1] Likewise, the word "Irish" refers to Scarlett's instinctive defensiveness and insecurity when she senses danger or uncertainty. When she confronts the self-assured, aristocratic taunting of Rhett Butler, "all the Irish in her rose to the challenge of his black eyes." (186) She perhaps knows that she is outmatched, but that doesn't mean that she'll surrender without a good fight.

Throughout *GWTW*, the condition of being Irish is seen by some white folks as barely above that of a slave. When Jonas Wilkerson, the former overseer at Tara, who is also of Yankee origin, wants to sting, he too uses the word "Irish" to "stereotype" Scarlett as nothing more than an uppity peasant. Thus, when she refuses to sell the Tara plantation to him, he uses what we would call today an "ethnic slur," calling the O'Hara family nothing but "bog-trotting Irish." (528) Even Scarlett herself distances herself from the common Irish laborers, who flock to Atlanta for work after the war, as when she refers to Johnnie Gallegher's workers as "that bunch of wild Irish." (735)

In one of the opening sequences of *GWTW*, the question of Irish blood is introduced as one of the major themes of the novel. When Gerald offers to carve out a nice farm from his land for Scarlett and whatever young man she decides to marry, whether Cade Calvert or one of the Tarleton or Munroe boys,

---

1. All quotes from *Gone With the Wind* in the present study are taken from the readily available Macmillan paperback edition, which is now distributed under the Avon Books imprint. To minimize the use of footnotes, page numbers will be indicated in the text.

his daughter rebukes him for talking like an Irishman. His response undergirds *GWTW*, and expresses one of the strongest convictions of the novel's authorial voice. It is abundantly clear, as far as Margaret Mitchell is concerned, that no matter what characters like Jonas Wilkerson or Rhett Butler in *GWTW* might say, it's okay to be Irish. Here is what Gerald O'Hara has to say about being Irish: "Have I ever been ashamed of it? No, 'tis proud I am. And don't be forgetting that you are half Irish, Miss! And to anyone with a drop of Irish blood in them the land they live on is like their mother. 'Tis ashamed of you I am this minute. I offer you the most beautiful land in the world - saving County Meath in the Old Country - and what do you do? You sniff!" (39)

As we see, Mitchell attributes to the Irish race, expelled from their own country by a harsh and heartless conqueror, a desire for land that they can call their own. To be Irish in *GWTW* is to be without pretension and to know your relatively minor place in this world. But that place cannot be adequately defined without land of one's own. The link between Irish identity and land in *GWTW* is developed further in Chapter 2.

As a cynic and a Satan figure, Rhett Butler is not terribly friendly to the Irish. In fact, he is the principal vehicle in *GWTW* for the denigration of the Irish race. He does this in two ways: either by insulting either Scarlett or her father for possessing a supposedly negative Irish trait, or by lambasting the Irish in general. As an example of the first instance, Rhett attacks Scarlett as someone who lacks a knowledge of the social nuances and delicacies that are standard fare in the planter class into which he was born. Thus, he can say to her when he suspects that she is not telling him the truth: "The Irish are among the poorest liars in the world. Come now, be frank." (616) The Irish are also prone to temper tantrums, speaking out before weighing their words. Rhett expresses this idea when he says to Scarlett: "No, it is one of my most priceless memories - a delicately nurtured Southern belle with her Irish up - You are very Irish, you know." (195) Being Irish also connotes expressing one's thoughts directly. When Scarlett asks Rhett to keep his mouth shut and not say so many unpatriotic things about the Cause, he replies: "That's your system, isn't it, my green eyed hypocrite? Scarlett, Scarlett! I hoped for more courageous conduct from you. I thought the Irish said what they thought and the Divvil take the hindmost. Tell me truthfully, don't you sometimes almost burst from keeping your mouth shut?" (236) And if the Irish usually express their thoughts directly, it is because they are less civilized, being much closer to the peasant experience. As Rhett tells Scarlett: "No, I don't love you. but I do like you tremendously - for the elasticity of your conscience, for the selfishness which you seldom trouble to hide, and for the shrewd practicality in you, which, I fear, you get from some not too remote Irish-peasant ancestor." (335) Later, along the same lines, even Will Benteen echoes Rhett when he tells Scarlett: "Now don't fly off the handle and get your Irish up." (684) Finally, Rhett also reserves the right to deride Scarlett by insulting her father, as when he refers to Gerald as "nothing but a smart Mick on the make." (891) Gerald might have accumulated wealth, but he is still uncivilized in Rhett's eyes.

In the second instance, Rhett does not hesitate to damn the Irish people as a whole. Thus, he shows no sympathy for the memory that the Irish have of their collective racial sufferings. Speaking of the Irish who were starved to death by Cromwell at the siege of Drogheda in 1649, he expresses his contempt for these uncivilized people, telling her that he couldn't care less about "the exotic viands the Irish ate at the siege." (303) And as for Irish taste in general, which is definitely limited by their peasant background and uncouth manners, Rhett has this to say: "There's no accounting for tastes, and I've always heard the Irish were partial to pigs." (304) Even Gerald's and Scarlett's obsession with owning land comes under fire from Rhett, for he sees this attachment as a pathology. "The Irish," he said. . . , "are the damnedest race. They put so much emphasis on so many wrong things. Land, for instance." (574)

Each of these examples highlights a supposedly negative Irish racial trait. They are used in the novel to reflect the widely held view in polite 19th century American society that the Irish were barbarians. Yet, despite these put downs, the authorial voice of *GWTW* does not hide its sympathy for Scarlett. Since the Irish have blended into mainstream society in the past 30 years, these negative remarks can tend to seem a bit antiquated. We can better appreciate the sting and venom in these verbal assaults if we substitute for the word "Irish" one of the terms that designates politically protected groups in contemporary society.

Mitchell's "stereotyping" of the Irish

Do these quotes from the text of *GWTW* mean that Margaret Mitchell was "anti-Irish?" Can it be said that she is guilty of "stereotyping" the Irish in *GWTW*.? This is not an idle question, for the Irish, from the time of the massive immigrations of the 1840's until just before World War II, were outcasts in the eyes of the American social elites. The Irish "race," as the term is used by Rhett Butler in *GWTW*, was considered to be different from and inferior to, other races, especially the dominant Anglo-Saxon one. They were kept out of what we call today the "mainstream" in a number of ways, and were perpetually reminded that they were not fully American - no matter how long their ancestors had lived in this country. They were "different," so different in fact that they were routinely portrayed in newspaper cartoons during these years as apes and gorillas. Paul Goldberger made this point clearly in his review of the exhibit "Gaelic Gotham: A History of the Irish in New York," which was organized by the Museum of the City of New York in 1996. "For three-quarters of a century after their heavy wave of immigration began in the mid-1800's, the Irish in New York were generally treated as a low, and sometimes even untouchable, class." [2] The same statement can be made about the Irish throughout the rest of the country as well. Their Catholicism marked them as foreign in a special way, but it was their 19th century penchant for alcohol abuse and street fighting that was perhaps most frowned upon by the nation's social elites. They were known as "the fighting Irish," and seemed to the "native Americans" of that day to be always ready to argue and riot over nothing. The adoption of this nickname by the Notre Dame football team in the 1920s, at the same time that Mitchell was writing *GWTW*, drips with irony. Although this gesture was a reminder of the days when official WASP culture systematically derided the American Irish, as well as a signal that things

---

2. Paul Goldberger, "How the Irish Came, and Overcame," *The New York Times,* March 15, 1996, pp. B1, B14.

were already getting better for them by that time, they were still not totally accepted. It's sobering to remember that terms like "paddy wagon," "hooligan" and "hooliganism," which are still often repeated in the press, would have been dropped long ago if they derided the media-protected groups that have political clout.

I mention these facts in order to provide perspective on the comments of those who see *GWTW* as a "racist" book that attacks black people and celebrates some mythical "Southern way of life." As we see from the example of the Irish, Mitchell allows certain characters to say some things with which she certainly does not agree. She does so for the simple reason that people who lived in that day and age actually said and believed such things. And this is precisely why her book has been so successful: it is historically accurate and internally consistent. Thus, those who take offense at this or that passing remark in *GWTW* about a black character or black folks in general, should recall that the Irish also take their lumps in precisely the same way in *GWTW*. And in neither case does Mitchell necessarily agree with what any character, or the novel's authorial voice, which generally mirrors Scarlett's views, might say. In fact, we know that she felt deep affection for both negroes, as blacks were called in those days, and the Irish. To damn the novel because it is judged to be politically incorrect by *today's* standards, applying *today's* speech codes to speech patterns that prevailed in the middle third of the last century, when no such restrictions existed, is patently unfair. At the same time, such readers and commentators, failing to see the larger picture, ignore the "ethnic slurs" that various characters in *GWTW* hurl at the Irish, whether as a group, or as individuals.

Physical Characteristics of the Irish

There can be no doubt that Margaret Mitchell identified with and admired particular Irish traits. These included certain physical characteristics, which she found pleasing. The most notable of these are perhaps red hair and fair skin, which she and her mother shared. It has been said many times that the Celts of Ireland, the so-called Milesians, were a race of black-haired, fair-skinned and blue-eyed people. Then, with the Norman conquest of the coastal areas of Ireland in the eleventh century, red hair was introduced into Ireland. Coming from Scandinavia via France, where they had been settled for several generations, the Normans gradually intermarried with the Milesians. As they were absorbed as a part of the Irish race, red hair became an additional Irish trait.

This point is very important since Mitchell was very conscious of the fact that the Fitzgeralds, of which she was one, were descended from these Norman conquerors of Ireland. In Ireland, the patronymics, "O" [descendant of] and "Mc" [son of] designate the indigenous Milesian race of Gaels, who have lived there since the beginning of recorded history, while the Normans had their own patronymic designation, "Fitz," from the French *fils,* for son, and used it as a prefix for their names. Thus, red hair in Irish history is associated with the Normans, and Margaret Mitchell was quite conscious of the Norman origins of her great grandfather Fitzgerald's name.

I wrote these words before being fortunate enough to come across a copy of an unpublished letter that Mitchell wrote to a relative in 1947. In answer to this relative, who wanted to learn more about the family origins of the Fitzgerald/Stephens clan, she demonstrated once again her detailed knowledge of Irish history.[3]

> In your second letter to me you evidenced an ignorance of the fact that Fitzgerald was an Irish name, and wrote that it sounded Scotch. It is one of the oldest and proudest of all Norman-Irish names, and one of the most famous. It is so famous that it was concerning the Fitzgeralds that the well known adage, long passed into the folklore of the world, was written - "Hibernicus ipsis Hibernior" ("For they became more Irish than the Irish themselves"). Fitzgerald is a Norman-Irish name, the "Fitz" being a corruption of the French prefix "fils". The Geraldines were a family of knights who lived in Tuscany. When William the Conqueror set out to invade England, adventurers from all

3. I am indebted to Mrs. Fontaine Le Maistre of Jacksonville, Florida, for permitting me to quote from this letter, and to Noëlle King, Principal Researcher at Margaret Mitchell House, Inc., in Atlanta, for bringing it to my attention.

the known world flocked to join him, hoping to make their fortunes. The Fitzgeralds went into England in 1066. Some sixty or more years later, they went into Ireland with the invading forces under Strong Bow. The Normans apportioned out the lands of the Irish, believing they could hold the country by these small overlords. But, for the most part, the Irish married their conquerors and little time passed before all Ireland was in arms against the sons of William the Conqueror. When questions were asked about the Fitzgeralds and why they were in the field leading the Irish against the Norman-Irish kings, the rueful and indignant statement was made to the King of England that the Fitzgeralds had become more Irish than the Irish themselves. Through a great many centuries they have fought for their country, and history is studded with the great names of Fitzgeralds. . ."

This passage speaks eloquently about Margaret Mitchell's knowledge of, and identification with, Irish history. Is it any wonder that the Irish theme is written into the text of *GWTW* with such authority?

In the novel, the physical features of the Norman-Irish are commemorated in the character of Beatrice Tarleton and her eight red-headed children. Mitchell associates the color red with this character, who has red hair, "russet eyes," (698) eight red-headed children, and rides a red mare, named Nellie. "Frail, fine-boned, so white of skin that her flaming hair seemed to have drawn all the color from her face into its vital burnished mass, she was nonetheless possessed of exuberant health and untiring energy. She had borne eight children, as red of hair and as full of life as she..." (87) Her very name, Beatrice, which designates the ideal woman who inspired Dante in his literary quest as he wrote *The Divine Comedy*, serves to reinforce the character's physical beauty. Each of her four daughters possesses a different shade of red hair. Among them are "Hetty's plain red hair, Camilla's strawberry blonde, Randa's coppery auburn and small Betsy's carrot top." (89)

But all is not rosy among the Irish, for there are also several less than desirable physical traits in the gene pool. The one that Mitchell focusses on is shortness of stature, as portrayed in two male characters, Gerald O'Hara and Johnnie Gallegher. They are anything but tall, aristocratic types, whether they be of light or dark complexion, like Ashley or Rhett. Their physical "disability" is no doubt intended to underline their plebian, indeed peasant, origins. Of course, Mitchell herself was also quite short. Furthermore, Gerald and Johnnie have no educational background and must get by on their wits. In this, too, they are both very much like Margaret Mitchell at one point in her life. After all, when she landed her first job as a journalist in 1923, she didn't have much of a resumé. Although she had been an underachiever in high school, had completed only one year of college, and (if one believes the story that she touted later on, after the success of *GWTW*) felt that she had disappointed her mother who had wanted her to become a doctor, she landed this first position on the basis of her grit and determination, or "gumption."

Gerald, the youngest of six brothers, is only five feet four and a half inches tall, while his five older brothers, like their father, are all over six feet in height. But more importantly, "he never wasted regrets on his lack of height and never found it an obstacle to his acquisition of anything he wanted. Rather, it was Gerald's compact smallness that made him what he was, for he had learned early on that little people must be hardy to survive among large ones. And Gerald was hardy." (45-6) If Margaret Mitchell had had to write her own obituary, these words about Gerald might very well have been included in it.

Johnnie Gallegher, the other little Irishman of *GWTW*, is the counterpoint to Gerald's blustery and somewhat uncivilized goodness. To Frank Kennedy, who derides him as a low class individual, Johnnie is nothing but "shanty Irish on the make." (753) [We recall that this is the same thing that Rhett says about Gerald. (891)] Physically, Johnnie has "short bowed legs," and "a gnomish face hard and businesslike." (753) He is a rather unsavory Irishman, but despite this fact Scarlett has great respect for his ability to get things done. But why does the author stress that he is a gnome, an imaginary dwarf-like creature who lives underground, where he hordes his treasure? Of all the characters of *GWTW*, Johnnie stands out as being the most physically repulsive. No black character in the novel is portrayed this way. Yet Johnnie is able to accomplish his objectives by dint of hard work and discipline, virtues he shares with Scarlett. "She knew that an Irishman with a determination to get somewhere was a valuable man to have, regardless of what his personal characteristics might be. And she felt a closer kinship with him than with many men of her own class, for Johnnie knew the value of money." Later, when Scarlett learns that Johnnie lives at her mill with "a fat mulatto woman" (776) named Rebecca (777), she simply looks the other way, for this is none of her business. She'll take Johnnie just the way he is.

The Irish Love of Horses

Beatrice Tarleton, in addition to possessing the Norman-Irish racial trait of red hair, also reflects the love that the Irish have for horses. She not only travels to Kentucky to make purchases, she also knows how to mate her animals in order to obtain the desired results. Perhaps the best proof that she is an emblem of certain Irish physical characteristics is the fact that her love for horses is shared by the two principal Irish-born characters of *GWTW*, Gerald O'Hara and Johnnie Gallegher. When we first meet Scarlett's father in *GWTW*, he is riding his horse back home in the late afternoon, jumping fences despite the dangers involved. And when he dies, it is a riding accident that takes his life. The connection between Beatrice Tarleton and Gerald in the matter of horses is underlined when Beatrice remarks at Gerald's funeral that "he was the only man in the County who knew a stallion from a gelding." (697)

Like Gerald, Johnnie Gallegher is also not only "little," he is also an "ex-jockey." (753) Despite Scarlett's recognition of his business sense, his coarseness is such that she still cannot imagine him riding a horse: "Whoever let him ride their horses didn't care much for horse flesh. I wouldn't let him get within ten feet of any horse of mine." (753) Of course, this same concern about horses had already been expressed by Beatrice Tarleton when she refused to give any of her fine horses to the Troop from the County when they were getting ready to go off to war in 1861. She was horrified by the thought that a Cracker, unskilled in horsemanship, might mistreat one of them. Then, after the war, when her four boys have been killed and all her horses slaughtered, Grandma Fontaine can say of her: "I don't know which hit Beetrice [sic] Tarleton worse, losing her boys or her horses." (706)

The Irish Affinity for Hard Work

Beyond the physical attributes of the Irish and their love for horses, Mitchell also recognizes their affinity for hard work. In the 19th century, it was the Irish who played the major role in digging the canals and building the railroads, their pride and their poverty forcing them to accept such outrageous economic exploitation without protest. "I never saw a lazy Irishman yet," Scarlett observes, (746) and in this she surely speaks for Margaret Mitchell. Mitchell had special admiration for those Irish *in her family* who had shown "gumption" and been successful in the struggle for economic survival. Among these one would surely have to include her immigrant great grandfather, Philip Fitzgerald. Thanks to his pluck and determination, he started with nothing in the 1830's and built Rural Home into a plantation of enviable size. According to the Fitzgerald genealogy contained in the *History of Clayton County*, he owned 2,375 acres and 35 slaves by 1854. [4]

On the subject of the Irish and hard work, a few more words are in order here about Johnnie Gallegher. When Scarlett first catches sight of him, he is in the background "among the rough Irish masons who were laying the foundation" (629) of a building while she talks to Tommy Wellburn. Then, when she meets Johnnie, he is described as "the foreman of the Irish workers, a hard-bitten little gnome of a man who had a very bad reputation." (629) He surely knows how to work hard, but even more so, he knows how to get the most out of those who are under his control. An Irish-born veteran of the Union Army, he has settled in Atlanta after the war to seek his fortune. Since he is successful in supervising gangs of Irish laborers on construction projects, Scarlett hires him to run one of her saw mills and he does

---

4. Joseph Henry Hightower Moore, *History of Clayton County*, Jonesboro, GA: Ancestors Unlimited, 1983, p. 242.

so with great success, turning a profit for her month after month. Then, when Scarlett decides to use convict labor, he shows no scruple for he thinks that he understands what she is trying to do: maximize profit by reducing labor costs and human compassion to a minimum. Thus, we are told that after Johnnie replaces Hugh Elsing as the supervisor at the sawmill, "he accomplished more with five convicts than Hugh had ever done with his crew of ten free negroes." (753) Scarlett admires his ability to accomplish his goals, especially at a time in life when she has turned her back on the Catholic ideals that her mother had inculcated in her.

In summary, Mitchell devotes more energy to describing the Irish in *GWTW* than she does to any other group of people. Her balance sheet includes certain positive attributes, but they are balanced by her sharp eye for defects.

Chapter 2:
Rural Home/Fontenoy Hall/Tara

Margaret Mitchell's Great Aunts

It all began with Margaret Mitchell's many visits as a girl with her mother to the Fitzgerald family homestead in Clayton County. Her mother's two maiden aunts, Mary Ellen Fitzgerald (1840-1926) and Sarah Fitzgerald (1849-1928), still lived there. These two women, who have not received much more than passing mention from Mitchell's biographers, actually play a key role in the genesis of *GWTW*. Margaret Mitchell evokes her debt to her great aunts, who represented the oral link to Ireland, when she writes of Gerald: "There were too many Irish ancestors crowding behind Gerald's shoulders, men who had died on scant acres, fighting to the end rather than leave homes where they had lived, plowed, loved, begotten sons." (404) Like Gerald, Mitchell's Irish ancestors "crowded" behind her. Her challenge was to retell to a new generation the stories passed down to her by the great aunts.

"Aunt Mamie" and her sister, called "Aunt Sis," "Sadie," "Sally," or "Miss Sarah Jane," were a tangible link with the antebellum era. They had been born on the family plantation before the war and had lived through the war years as girls. They were as staunchly faithful to Catholicism as any two people could be in that day and age, and this commitment was matched by a nostalgia for the old days before the Yankee invaders had come to destroy their way of life. The article devoted to them in the *History of Clayton County*[5] is most informative and, for our purposes, documents important points of contact between them and their sister's granddaughter, Margaret Mitchell. They lived in their father's house, Rural Home, which he himself had bought in the 1820's, until their deaths. They were still planting cotton on their farm when they

5. pp. 243-4.

were in their seventies, while renting out other parcels of their acreage to tenant farmers. The Fitzgerald farm no longer exists, but the plantation house, Rural Home, can still be seen. It was rescued from destruction thanks to Betty Talmadge in the 1980's. Already in an advanced state of disrepair, it was moved to her property at Lovejoy Plantation, where it can still be seen today.

"Aunt Sis," in particular, exercised a powerful effect on young Margaret, for she was still a beautiful woman in advanced age. Some people said that her beau had been killed in the war, but that no one would dare to ask her about it. This theme is of course recycled by Mitchell in her novel, for losing a beau in the war was no laughing matter, as exemplified by India Wilkes. But it was one thing to be embittered by this experience, like India, and another to overcome it. Aunt Sis's natural graciousness was also legendary. "It was said of her that she could rise from her seat on her back porch with a pan of snapbeans in her hand and receive the King of England or the Pope of Rome in the gracious and proper manner called for." (243) This trait was passed on to the character of Melanie in GWTW who, despite the humble circumstances of her one story brick house on Ivy Street in Atlanta, received all with dignity. From Archie, the wife killer, to Fr. Ryan, the poet-priest of the Confederacy, to Alexander "Little Alec" Stephens, the first and only Vice President of the Confederacy, all fell under the spell of her graciousness. The natural gentility of "Aunt Sis" is immortalized in this aspect of Melanie's character.

During Reconstruction, Aunt Sis had one of the two-room guesthouses on the Fitzgerald property lifted off its foundation and rolled down the road. Here she used it as a school house for negro children. She gave lessons in reading and writing there until the U. S. Freedmen's Bureau, "wishing to make the cleavage between ex-slaves and ex-masters as wide and as bitter as possible, made it too unpleasant for her to continue." (243) This experience with Yankee arrogance becomes a major theme in the second half of GWTW. In particular, the authorial voice of the novel expresses special contempt for the work of the Freedmen's Bureau, which becomes an emblem of Northern hypocrisy.

Fontenoy Hall

When Mitchell began writing *GWTW* in 1926, she had in her mind a clear vision of the many days, weeks and months she had spent with her great aunts in Clayton County. Until the end of 1928, she used the name Fontenoy Hall to describe the transposed Fitzgerald property at Rural Home. Anne Edwards, in *The Road to Tara,* tells us that "she was not entirely satisfied with this name, but it was of her own making and she wanted to be sure that no plantation in Clayton County could be identified."[6] This statement is literally true, but it is also misleading in so far as it implies that the term was a mere invention that Mitchell had arbitrarily selected. In telling us that Mitchell's main reason for selecting it was her concern that someone might sue her if she used the name of a plantation that had actually existed, Edwards is also technically correct, but this explanation still leaves out too much. This is because the word Fontenoy had enormous implications for the Irish people in the middle of the 19th century - and particularly for those Irish who went abroad in search of a better life. Fontenoy is first of all the name of a place, a plateau outside the city of Tournai in Belgium, just beyond the French border. But to the 19th century Irish, whether at home or in the diaspora, it had enormous symbolic value. In fact, those three syllables were sacred to them in that they evoked a great French victory over England and her allies in 1745 during the War of the Austrian Succession. In this battle, the French fought the combined armies of Holland, England, and the Hanoverian/Austrian dynasties. Under the leadership of the German-born Maurice of Saxony, and in the presence of King Louis XV himself, the French army went into battle. But several hours later, they seemed to be losing. The English infantry had broken through their lines and were still advancing. Was France, which had not been able to defeat the English in the field since the 14th century, going to be vanquished once more? Not to worry. At this critical moment, Maurice of Saxony committed his elite units, the crack troops of his Irish Brigades, which had been held in reserve for just such an occasion. These Irish mercenaries, who gladly fought for France as a way to show their hatred for England and her exploitation of their homeland, now moved

6. Anne Edwards, *The Road to Tara.* New York, Dell, 1984, p. 135.

forward. They advanced into withering British fire. But, as historian Joseph G. Bilby tells us in his remarkable book, *Remember Fontenoy! The 69th New York and the Irish Brigade in the Civil War,* the French victory "was owed to an unstoppable bayonette charge by the French army's brigades of Irish exiles." Despite heavy losses, the Irish forced the English and their allies to retreat. It was a victory that France still savors to this day.

One can judge what this victory meant to Louis XV by the unprecedented rewards that he showered upon his Irish troops. Not only did he ride down the line and tell them directly that he owed his victory to them, something that no "absolute monarch" had ever done before, he also showered them with tangible rewards that included promotions, pensions and Crosses of Saint Louis for valor in the field. In addition, one of the trophies that fell into Louis XV's hands as a result of his victory at Fontenoy was put to special use. Taking possession of the wealthy city of Ghent, a center of the weaving trades, he confiscated the vast storehouses of cloth that the British had stockpiled there and ordered that new uniforms be made for the members of the Irish Brigades.

Thereafter, for at least the next century, the word Fontenoy resonated on Irish lips with enormous symbolic value. It meant that "the wild geese,"[8] as the Irish mercenaries who fought for France in those days were called, were every bit as valiant as their English counterparts, and that, if given an even chance to go against them one on one, could defeat them on the field of battle. But it also meant that the Irish, no matter where they might be, and however far from Erin's shores, were still Irish. And most especially when they dealt a solid blow against Old England.

We can gauge the power of the word Fontenoy for the Irish in America when we recall the recruiting efforts that were undertaken in New York when the 69th New York Regiment, the so-called "Fighting Irish" of Civil War fame (and later, in World War I, and World War II), was first organized in 1861. One had only to sound the words "Remember Fontenoy!" and the Irish recruits came flooding in.

This planned use of the term Fontenoy by Margaret Mitchell is yet another eloquent and tangible proof of her extensive and detailed knowledge of Irish social and military history. But

---

7. Hightstown, NJ: Longstreet House Books, 1995. p.5.

8. This is how they were listed on the manifests of the ships that brought them clandestinely from the wild west of Ireland to France.

even more importantly, the term authenticates the link to Rural Home, an architecturally humble and undistinguished farm house among many others in rural Clayton County, while also showing how Margaret Mitchell was beginning to see it in her imagination. She was about to give it, with the word Tara, the mythic dimension that millions of readers have come to accept in the last sixty years.

Tara

In 1928, the term Fontenoy Hall was changed to Tara, which has become the most widely known place name in American fiction. It is important to trace this further transformation of Rural Home, for it confirms Mitchell's consciousness of her Irish heritage.

"Yes, Tara was worth fighting for," (428) Scarlett discovers after the war, and she resolves to keep the plantation in the family. (428) Likewise, Mitchell, in writing her novel, was also keeping Rural Home alive and with it the memory of her Fitzgerald ancestors.

The word Tara refers to two separate but closely related entities. It is first of all a pre-historic man-made hill, or burial mound, located some 30 miles outside of Dublin in County Meath. Excavations carried out since World War II have located deep within the recesses of Tara a number of ritual or burial chambers. Was it here that living victims were sacrificed by the Druids to their sun god? On the longest day of the year, light passes though a shaft into one of these chambers, proving its use as a site of ritual.

The second meaning of the word refers more directly to *GWTW*. From the second to the sixth century, the area we call Tara, that is, the principal mound and others in the general vicinity, was the site of a dynasty of Irish kings, who ruled from their famous Hall of Assembly. Some scholars see a Roman influence in the traces of the building's foundations, but this is difficult to prove. As Padraic Colum has pointed out, "... around A. D. 200, [King] Cormac made Tara a social as well as a political center by building the great Hall of Assembly in which outstanding personages among the nobility and the learned classes were entertained during the sacred festivals; he also made the lesser kings lodge their youthful princes in Tara as hostages. It is possible that in Cormac's time there were influences from Roman Britain; some scholars see the famous Hall of Tara as a reproduction of a Roman building." [9]

Margaret Mitchell chose the word Tara as one of the clues that she wanted to pass along to future generations. It confirms that one of her goals in writing the novel was to commemorate the Irish blood that flowed in her veins.

It is significant that Mitchell decided to change the name of the O'Hara family plantation from Fontenoy Hall to Tara after attending her Aunt Sis's funeral in Fayetteville.[10] She returned home and immediately set to work describing Gerald O'Hara's funeral. The transformation that must have taken place in her mind is not too difficult to reconstruct. From Fontenoy Hall she was able to go directly to a one word name - like Mimosa for the Fontaines and Fairhill for the Tarletons - because she suddenly understood that the word "hall" is implied in Tara. But why is this?

It is highly likely that her inspiration for this change was provided by the example of the well-known poem by the Irish poet Thomas Moore, (1779-1852) entitled "The Harp That Once Through Tara's Halls." The poem's principal theme, the end of a civilization that only a work of literature can bring back, however fleetingly, fits snugly with what Mitchell herself was struggling to bring to life. She too wanted to resurrect the end of a world that no harp (the poetical symbol of the bard) will ever describe and celebrate again. She too was seeking at the time to be an Irish bard in the sense of the poem. Her harp, the Remington on which she worked in the Dump, was the instrument that she would use to bring Rural Home and the precious memories of her ancestors back to life. This also helps to explain why music and song are so important in *GWTW*, at least as long as Gerald O'Hara is alive. Her mother had sung Civil War songs to her from infancy and she knew them all by heart. As Anne Edwards observes, "... the early years of Margaret's life were heavily influenced by a war fought four decades earlier. She was taught the names of battles along with the alphabet, and Maybelle's lullabies were doleful Civil War songs." (21) The concept of a lost world was an intimate part of her

9. Padraic Colum, *A Treasury of Irish Folklore*, New York: Crown, 1954, p. 84.

10. *The Road to Tara*, pp. 146-47.

life. Thus, Moore's image of the harp of Tara must have impressed her.

Finally, how do we know that Mitchell even knew of Moore's work? Just so there would be no doubt about this, she also quoted another one of Moore's poems, "The Lament for Robert Emmet," in the text of *GWTW*. It is discussed in detail in Chapter 5 of the present study. Here now is the text of "The Harp That Once through Tara's Halls."

> The harp that once through Tara's halls
>   The soul of music shed,
> Now hangs as mute on Tara's walls
>   As if that soul were fled.
> So sleeps the pride of former days,
>   So glory's thrill is o'er,
> And hearts that once beat high for praise,
>   Now feel that pulse no more!

***

> No more to chiefs and ladies bright
>   The harp of Tara swells;
> The chord alone that breaks at night,
>   Its tale of ruin tells.
> Thus Freedom now so seldom wakes,
>   The only throb she gives
> Is when some heart indignant breaks,
>   To show that still she lives.

Mitchell's Irish Obsession: the Land

As an adult, Margaret Mitchell never owned her own home. After her marriage to John Marsh on the Fourth of July in 1925, they took up residence in the large house that Cornelius Sheehan, who had been a member of Sacred Heart Parish in the early years of the 20th century and the head of one of the most prominent families in the parish, had built for his family in 1899. The Sheehan and Stephens families, both very active in the parish, were friends. By the mid 20's, the neighborhood was changing. The area around Tenth and Peachtree, no longer predominantly residential, was becoming more commercial. Thus, the Sheehan house had been transformed into an apartment building.

John Marsh and Peggy Mitchell moved in on the ground floor, taking the apartment that she would later immortalize as "the Dump," or "the Dump on Tight Squeeze," as the intersection of Tenth and Peachtree was called. They would live there for the first seven years of their marriage, and it was there that she would write her great novel. This apartment has been restored by Margaret Mitchell House, Inc., to resemble its appearance when *GWTW* was being written. But even later, after her success, the Marshes continued to rent, in part because they didn't want people to say that they were showing off their wealth. But of course there were other reasons as well. Not only did they both suffer from ill health, they were also so totally involved in their work that it is difficult to imagine how they would have found the time to maintain a house.

Yet, *GWTW* demonstrates that the cult of the land was in Mitchell's blood. When Scarlett returns to Tara in 1864, she has just missed seeing her mother one more time, for Ellen had died the previous day. [This, of course, replicates Mitchell's own experience when she too returned home the day after her mother's death.] The place thus takes on the aura of a site of religious pilgrimage for her. She cannot and will not give it up for it is not only bound up with the love of the land that Gerald has bequeathed to her, but also with her guilty feelings for not having lived up to her mother's teachings and admonitions. When she recalls that Yankees had actually ransacked the house, "a feeling that the beloved walls had been defiled rose in her. This house, sacred because Ellen had lived in it..." (403) must be preserved. And the obsession to hold on to Tara is to be acted out in the name of all those who live there and depend upon her - including Pork, Mammy, Dilcey and Prissy.

And if she is now resolved to save Tara, it is because this idea has been latent in her from the beginning. One of the most memorable scenes in *GWTW* occurs early in the novel when Gerald suggests that Scarlett marry Cade Calvert, a young man of whom he approves, for then he would be able to leave Tara to him and Scarlett after his death. When Scarlett tells him that plantations don't amount to anything, he responds, and in so doing posits love of the land as one of the major themes of *GWTW*: "Land is the only thing in the world that amounts to anything... for 'tis the only thing in this world that lasts, and don't you be forgetting it! 'Tis the only thing worth working for, worth fighting for - worth dying for." (38-9) Later, in Atlanta, Scarlett finally understands what her father meant: "For the first time, she realized dimly what Gerald had meant when he said that the love of the land was in her blood." (154) Finally, after her return to Tara, and the shock of loss at seeing it devastated, she recalls once more the earlier conversation and determines to save Tara.

> As from another world she remembered a conversation with her father about the land and wondered how she could have been so young, so ignorant, as not to understand what he meant when he said that the land was the one thing in the world worth fighting for. "For 'tis the only thing in the world that lasts....and to anyone with a drop of Irish blood in them the land they live on is like their mother....'Tis the only thing worth working for, fighting for, dying for."(428)

We know that this theme was intentionally developed by Mitchell and did not come about by accident. In a letter to Gilbert Govan, who had reviewed *GWTW* in the *Chattanooga Times* on July 5, 1936, Mitchell wrote: "Thank you for your remark about Gerald who 'recognizes that security can never be found apart from the land.' No one else picked that up; no one seemed to think of it or notice it. And that depressed me for while I didn't hammer on it I meant it for an undercurrent. And I felt, as I suppose all authors are prone to feel, nine tenths of the time, that I had utterly failed in getting my ideas over."[11]

After the success of the film version of *GWTW*, Mitchell would correctly observe that her great grandfather's house, Rural Home, had been overdone in the Hollywood set. She conceived of the latter more as a pioneer's homestead built of "whitewashed brick," or with "white walls," (50) and presented

---

11. Richard Harwell, editor, *Margaret Mitchell's Gone With The Wind Letters, 1936-1949,* New York: Macmillan, 1976. p. 23.

it as such in the novel. The Tara of the novel, although it is built of brick and not pine, is thus much closer to Rural Home, the Fitzgerald homestead, than the Hollywood set turned out to be.

Chapter 3:
The Irish Mother, Grandmother, and Great Grandmother

May Belle and Margaret

Before Margaret Mitchell herself began spending summers at Rural Home, the ancestral Fitzgerald property in Clayton County, as well as making other visits during the course of the year, her mother, May Belle Stephens Mitchell (1872-1919), had had this same experience. Since May Belle's mother, Annie Fitzgerald Stephens, the sister of Mamie and Sis, was not known to be a nurturing mother, she availed herself of every possible opportunity to send her daughter off to the Fitzgerald farm in the country. There May Belle, intelligent and sensitive, spent long periods of time with her Fitzgerald aunts, "Mamie," and "Aunt Sis." It was from them that she acquired the Fitzgerald taste for book learning, and in particular for the Catholic tradition in art and literature. This, in turn, would be passed on to her daughter, Margaret.

Mitchell's biographers have stressed the idea of a lack of empathy between May Belle and her daughter. To Anne Edwards, for instance, in *The Road to Tara*, Mitchell is unfocused as a student and her mother is a cool, detached suffragette who remains aloof from her daughter. According to this analysis, May Belle plays psychological games with Margaret in order to achieve her ends, no matter how much damage this might do to the child. Then May Belle dies suddenly while her daughter is away at college. "All her life she had fought for her mother's approval, and her being at Smith and planning to be a doctor was part of that pattern." (59) Likewise, for Darden Asbury Pyron, in his *Southern Daughter,* theirs was a "conflicted relationship,"[12] from the beginning. It culminated in May Belle's sending her daughter away to Smith. Since May Belle saw the college as a place where a woman could be politically liberated, she unilaterally made the decision that her daughter

12. New York, Oxford University Press, 1991, p. 81

would go there. Margaret was sent off without asking her about her own preferences - and without even a campus visit by either mother or daughter. There is a good deal of truth in this some-what stark portrayal of the mother-daughter relationship, for May Belle, who married too young and seemed to be forever plagued with health problems, wanted to see her daughter achieve what she had not been able to do. But at the same time, this is hardly an unusual state of affairs in ambitious, middle class families.

To my mind, what is at question is the matter of degree. Did May Belle go too far? Did she do harm to her daughter in want-ing the best for her? In stressing this theme of conflict, which highlights the daughter's supposed inability to fulfill the moth-er's dreams for her, doesn't one run the risk of overlooking the deep complicity that undeniably existed between the two women? There is no doubt that their personalities were quite different, a difference accentuated by their difference in age and generation, but they were also linked by so many other strands of life: blood, extended family ties, and a shared view of the Southern past, to mention only a few.

In her will, Margaret Mitchell bequeathed many of her let-ters to the University of Georgia. Many, but not nearly all of them, have been published. Mitchell was already a faithful cor-respondent prior to becoming a celebrity, but once overtaken by fame, she became almost compulsive in this regard. She wrote literally thousands of missives in her lifetime, and was particu-larly active in this regard beginning in 1936 when people con-gratulated her on her success. Where and how, they wanted to know, did she learn so much about the Civil War era?

> I heard so much when I was little about the fighting and the hard times after the war that I firmly believed Mother and Father had been through it all instead of being born long after-ward. . . [13]

This tribute to the family oral tradition at home, in which she pays tribute to both her mother and her father, is touching, but a bit inaccurate. Mitchell's father, taciturn by nature and a lawyer by training, weighed his words and did not use them

13. Richard B. Harwell, editor, *Margaret Mitchell's Gone With the Wind Letters*, 1936-1949. New York: Macmillan, 1976. p. 3

lightly. It was actually May Belle who carried the load in this regard. This oral tradition within the immediate family was supplemented by visits to relatives. Here Mitchell invokes the heritage from both sides of her family:

> When we went calling on the older generation of relatives, those who had been active in the sixties, I sat on the bony knees of veterans and the fat slippery laps of great aunts and heard them talk about the times when Little Alex [Confederate Vice-President Stephens] was visiting them and how much fried chicken Father Ryan could put away and how nice thick wrapping paper felt when put between the skin and the corset in the cold days during the blockade when woolen goods were so scarce. And how Grandpa Mitchell walked nearly fifty miles after the battle of Sharpsburg with is skull cracked in two places from a bullet. They didn't talk of these happenings as history nor as remarkable events but just as a part of their lives and not especially epic parts. And they gradually became a part of my life. (Harwell, 4)

Of particular interest to us here are the references to "great aunts" and to "Father Ryan," two key figures in Mitchell's imaginative reconstruction of a bygone era. Each came to her through the mediation of her mother, who had begun the pilgrimages to Rural Home, where the Fitzgerald aunts lived, a generation before Margaret did.

Mitchell's transformation of her relationship with her mother is at the heart of *GWTW*. In accordance with her mother's wishes, Margaret had dutifully gone away to school and come home a day too late. Her mother was already dead when she returned to Atlanta. There had never been any formal closure in their relationship, and so much was left unsaid at the end! May Belle's premature death, and the circumstances in which it occurred, with her daughter so far away, had a powerful effect on Margaret. As a sensitive young woman who was aware of how difficult it is for two human beings to communicate effectively, Margaret perhaps decided at this time that she would never bear any children of her own. Why even try? Her own experience seemed to indicate how difficult it would be to attempt to communicate fully with any children she might eventually have. She also might have already suspected that she was not completely suited to this particular task.

But the question hounded her: how was she to bring closure to her relationship with her mother? How could she finally say those things that the force of circumstance had obliged her to leave unsaid? Their difference in temperament had been an obstruction during her mother's lifetime, but must it always be so? In a word, how could she finally express the love and admiration that she felt for her mother? And in so doing, how could she sing a hymn of praise to the Stephens and Fitzgeralds forebears whose legacy had been bequeathed to her through her mother? Gradually, between 1921 and 1925, the answers to these questions became apparent. She would express what had been left unsaid through the medium of fiction. Like Marcel Proust, she would resurrect her family's past - as well as that of an entire civilization - through a long, narrative work of art. All the things that mattered most to both mother and daughter would be expressed in this work.

Thus, Margaret Mitchell embarked on what would turn out to be the greatest novel in American fiction for rather private reasons. She wanted to set things right between herself and her mother, while at the same time paying homage to her ancestors. Mitchell would later say on several occasions that this was a completely private project, which she had no intention of ever publishing. We must not doubt her honesty and sincerity in this regard. But as the work progressed, it grew beyond her initial mental construct, literally taking on a life of its own. Once the genie was out of the bottle, there was no way of controlling it. On the contrary, it was the novel that took possession of its diminutive creator. As the novel developed, she began to fear that those close to her would be able to put the various pieces together. Thus, as the project was brought to completion about 1928, she found herself working more and more at cross purposes, trying to cover up as much as possible the personal and private inspiration that had made the work possible in the first place. From here on she became obsessed with the idea of keeping family and friends from seeing through her narrative. Having started to write the novel in order to show that she was indeed, to borrow Simone de Beauvoir's phrase, a "dutiful daughter,"[14] the last thing she now wanted was for the work, if it were ever read by anyone, to cause embarrassment to her family. This is why she later ordered that the various drafts of the novel be burned. Only a few chapters would be retained as proof that she, and not her husband, John Marsh, had written the novel. In this way she felt that it would be possible, after her death, to counter any naysayers who doubted her authorship (or at least said that they did), while also making sure that anything derogatory that she might have written about her only thinly-veiled relatives in various drafts of the work would be forever lost.

Eleanor McGhan and Margaret

The first thing that Mitchell did in mapping out *GWTW* was to transform the American-born, but Catholic side of her mother's family and give them French instead of Irish ancestry. How and why did she do this?

We recall that Mitchell's great grandfather, Philip Fitzgerald (1798-1880) had married Eleanor McGhan (1818-1893) about 1837. She was descended, according to family oral history, from Lord Calvert's original settlement in Maryland.[15] They had come with him on his ships, the Ark and the Dove, in 1634, and landed on St. Clement's Island in the Potomac. They then established their permanent settlement about twenty miles further south. Later, after the American Revolution, when freedom of religion became the law of the land, several of these families began to search for land in the South. They were especially attracted to Georgia, in the newly opened southeast frontier, where the practice of Catholicism had been specifically outlawed before the Revolution.

Thus, the McGhans were members of the original Catholic settlement at Locust Grove in Taliaferro County, Georgia, in 1793. As Catholics, they kept to the established tradition of

---

14. Simone de Beauvoir (1908-1986), *Memories of a Dutiful Daughter,* (Cleveland: World, 1959). Margaret Mitchell no doubt never heard of the French intellectual who is generally credited with being the principal precursor of the feminist movement. Beauvoir's seminal book, *The Second Sex,* appeared in French in 1949, the year of Mitchell's death, and only appeared in English translation in 1953. Yet there are striking similarities between the two women, which lack of space precludes me from exploring here. Each grew up in a traditional Catholic family and each rebelled against her milieu as a young woman, attaining international fame in the process.

15. I am indebted here, once again, to a *History of Clayton County.*

remaining separate from the rest of the population, farming the land, marrying among themselves, and not keeping slaves. In this way, they had managed to survive in Maryland for several generations and they were determined to follow the same formula in Georgia. The initial agricultural settlement at Locust Grove was so successful that within a generation their numbers had grown considerably. New lands were needed to provide farms for the burgeoning community. It was in this way that Eleanor McGhan's father acquired land in Morgan County, about 25 miles to the east. It was here, near Madison, that Eleanor McGhan was born in 1818.

Thus, the initial Locust Grove settlement saw the loss of some of its members in this outward migration. Since they were determined to earn their living as farmers and not as traders or manufacturers, many of them had to move in order to find adequate land. But the railroad had an even more far reaching effect on the Locust Grove settlement. In the years before the Civil War, the railroad ran a spur off the main line between Atlanta and Augusta. Its terminus was the colonial town of Washington, in Wilkes County, about fifteen miles to the north, but it passed through the crossroads called Sharon, located about a mile from Locust Grove. With the arrival of the railroad, times really began to change. The Locust Grove community could no longer maintain its isolation in the face of this revolutionary means of transportation. Thus, in order to be near the railroad, more and more members of the community moved to Sharon. Even the Catholic Church from Locust Grove, the first one ever built in the state of Georgia, was dismantled and moved to Sharon, where it still stands to this day.

Sadly, the original Catholic settlement of Margaret Mitchell's ancestors at Locust Grove is now completely abandoned. All that remains is the cemetery, next to which is the outline, in the form of several rockpiles, of the site upon which their church originally stood. It is located at the end of a dirt road running out of Sharon. The Georgia forest has reclaimed the land in the very same way that Scarlett, in *GWTW*, fears that Tara will be overgrown if it is abandoned and not kept up. One cannot make the pilgrimage to Locust Grove without asking oneself if Mitchell herself ever visited the place. My hunch is that she probably did. Land on which some of the world's best cotton was once grown by the Catholic pioneers of Locust Grove is now home to a melange of hardwoods and scrub pine.

Margaret Mitchell, with her Catholic ancestry running back to colonial Maryland, had a problem. She wanted to sing a hymn of praise to her mother's ancestors, but how was she to do this without having them "stereotyped" as Irish immigrants or, as Rhett Butler would say, "shanty Irish?" This role was already assigned to Gerald O'Hara and his family. The McGhans, although not "prominent" folk, were nonetheless "old" and "established" American families. They had pre-Revolutionary roots in the American soil. Mitchell's solution to her problem was to transform Eleanor McGhan's colonial heritage from the Irish to the French point on the Catholic spectrum. Thus, McGhan becomes Robillard, while Eleanor becomes Ellen. But why did Mitchell spell her name Ellen and not Hélène, which would have been the logical thing to do? After all, the names of her sisters, Eulalie and Pauline, of her cousin Philippe, and of her parents, Solange and Pierre, are all visibly French. Ellen is glaringly inconsistent with all these French given names! The answer is readily apparent: Mitchell called her character *Ellen* and not *Hélène* because she didn't want to dilute her testimony to the "gumption" of her Irish and Catholic great grandmother. So it was Ellen and not Hélène, however oddly the name pairs with Robillard.

The trap into which Anne Edwards falls is a good illustration of the pitfalls involved in reconstructing the relationship between Mitchell's family in fact and in fiction. In her at times insightful biography of Mitchell, she attributes French Huguenot ancestry to Mitchell's mother's family.[16] She seems to have believed that the Robillards were emblematic of genuine French ancestry on Mitchell's mother's side. The reality, of course, is that Margaret Mitchell was thoroughly Irish on May Belle's side.

In *GWTW*, Ellen Robillard is the daughter of a "French mother, whose parents had fled Haiti in the revolution of 1791." (42) In the novel she represents the coastal aristocracy. In physical appearance, she is "creamy skinned," with "slanting dark eyes, shadowed by inky lashes," black hair... and a "long straight nose." Finally, she has a "...square cut jaw that was softened by the gentle curving of her cheeks." (42) There is nothing here

---

16. In *Road to Tara,* she tells us that "her mother's family had immigrated to Charleston about 1685, after the Huguenot troubles in France..." (p. 15) Although this is not true, it sounds so much more refined to be of French Huguenot and not Irish Catholic ancestry!

that would make us think of May Belle. As for her dowry upon her marriage to Gerald O'Hara, Ellen brought Mammy and 20 "house niggers" (57) to her union. Was this detail based on family oral history?

The recently discovered and as yet unpublished letter that Margaret Mitchell sent to a cousin in 1947, mentioned above in Chapter 1, also sheds light on this subject. It has to do with family history and goes into a number of matters that are related to our concerns here. It also helps to explain how Anne Edwards went wrong on this point.

In answer to her relative's question about the origins of the McGhan family, Mitchell tells her outright: "The McGhans were not Scotch Presbyterians. The name is the most Irish of all Irish names, and has been a Catholic name as long as the records run. You asked, if McGhan was a Scotch Presbyterian name, how did Catholicism enter the clan? This question has me somewhat confused because, as far as any records in your family go, on your mother's side, your people have never been anything except Catholics. Every branch, even the most distant collateral, were Catholic, even the far-off Spanish line. You will forgive me if I do appear confused, but I cannot understand where you get the idea that your people were Scottish when they were all so proud of their Irish Catholic ancestry and never missed an opportunity to boast about it."

In this letter Mitchell also speaks about her family's Haitian French connection that she never mentioned anywhere else, as far as I have been able to determine. "However, my mother was Uncle Frank McGhan's [brother of Eleanor McGhan, May Belle's grandmother] favorite grandniece, and he spoke to her of his wife's people. I always heard they were of Haitian French descent. The coast towns from Key West to Charleston were full of these refugees." So now we finally know where Mitchell got the idea to transpose the McGhans from an Irish Catholic to a French Catholic background: she found it in her family history!

There was a disparity in age of some twenty years between Eleanor McGhan and Philip Fitzgerald. In those days, an ambitious man of humble origins needed time to amass sufficient wealth before assuming the responsibility of a family. Margaret Mitchell took these basic elements of the family history and transformed them as follows. The age disparity of twenty years between Philip Fitzgerald and his frontier bride is amplified to more than 25 years between Ellen and Gerald of *GWTW*. Their respective ages, about 20 and 40, are modified at the extremes, with Ellen dropping to 16 and Gerald rising to 43. But why? Was this an arbitrary change? Of course not. Mitchell had to make this age change in her great grandmother's marriage age for a very good reason: she wanted to develop the theme of the girl who falls in love at the age of 16 and enters a convent when marriage to the object of her affection becomes impossible. This theme is studied in detail in Chapter 7, below.

Finally, Eleanor and Philip Fitzgerald had seven children, four of whom, including two boys, died in infancy: Philip, Jr.; John Francis; Louise Burke; and Laetitia. Only the three girls, Annie, who will become Margaret Mitchell's grandmother, and her two sisters, Aunt Mamie and Aunt Sis, survive into adulthood. Likewise, in *GWTW*, Gerald and Ellen's first three children, all sons, die in infancy and are buried in the family cemetery at Tara. The three girls, all born later, survive. They are emblematic of the three Fitzgerald sisters.

Annie Fitzgerald and Margaret

Annie Fitzgerald Stephens (1844-1934) played a major role in Margaret Mitchell's life. She was nothing less than what the French call "une force de la nature." Imperious and strong-willed, she seemed to be forever set on getting her own way, and usually did. She was her parents' third child, after Mary Ellen (1840-1926), who never married, and Philip, Jr., (1842-1843) who died in infancy. In 1863, she married Irish-born John Stephens in Immaculate Conception Church in Atlanta, while he was on furlough from his duties as a Captain with the 9th Georgia Infantry.

His service in the Confederate Cause is memorialized in *GWTW*. When Will Benteen returns to Tara from a trip to Fayetteville, he tells Scarlett and Melanie that he "found somthin' right cute that I thought would interest you ladies and I brought it home." (506) It's a Confederate bill with a strip of brown wrapping paper pasted to the back, on which a poem has been written. The poem is called "Lines on the Back of a Confederate Note." (507)

> Representing nothing on God's earth now
> And naught in the waters below it -
> As the pledge of nation that's passed away,
> Keep it, dear friend, and show it.

> Show it to those who will lend an ear
> To the tale this trifle will tell
> Of Liberty, born of patriots' dream,
> Of a storm-cradled nation that fell.

These "lines" were not introduced into the text of *GWTW* by accident, but were put there because they had been written by Mitchell's maternal grandfather, John Stephens. Once again, we see the Fitzgerald/Stephens family legacy fertilizing and enriching the novel.

John Stephens (1833-1896) was born in King's County near Tipperary, and came directly to Georgia as a young man where he joined a brother who was a tradesman in Augusta. After his service in the war, he settled first in Fayette County and then relocated to Atlanta in 1872. He prospered during Reconstruction because he had a head for numbers and was skilled at bookkeeping. For these services he was able to earn hard cash at a time when that commodity was generally scarce. With the help of Annie, he invested his money in real estate, eventually becoming heavily involved in the development of the east side of the city of Atlanta. The center of his empire of rental properties ran along Jackson Street, a north-south artery that parallels Peachtree Street, about a mile to the east. He even founded his own trolley line, the Gate City Railway Company, to serve the area he had developed. After his death, Annie actively managed their properties for decades, and many said that she showed much more interest in real estate than in her children. The Fitzgerald/Stephens holdings in the neighborhood are still commemorated to this day by an artery known as Fitzgerald Street.

Annie Fitzgerald was the principal inspiration for the character of Scarlett O'Hara, whose name, we recall, is taken from her Irish ancestors, the Scarletts. (414) Both were born about the same time, Scarlett in 1844 and Annie in 1845, and both were teen brides during the Civil War, marrying officers. Each later became a domineering, grasping and possessive person, obsessed with land and property to the detriment of family considerations.

After May Belle's death, Margaret and her grandmother, so much alike, quarreled fiercely. There was no way that these two women could live under the same roof at 1401 Peachtree Street. Thus, Annie decamped to the Georgian Terrace Hotel with the intention of living there permanently.

Margaret Mitchell told people without batting an eyelash that she couldn't stand her grandmother. This was no doubt true. Yet she admired her tremendously for her "gumption." To the extent that Annie wouldn't let anybody trample on her, Margaret had to begrudgingly give her credit for this most "modern" trait in a woman born before the Civil War.

It was truly a stroke of genius to build so many of her grandmother's character traits into Scarlett O'Hara, adding complexity to what would have otherwise been a relatively transparent autobiographical novel based on Margaret and May Belle's relationship. Thus, as Mitchell wrote her novel, she attributed to Scarlett what she took to be her grandmother's most negative characteristics: her unladylike behavior, especially her combativeness; her desire to overlook nothing, answering even the smallest perceived slight; her obsession with land and property; and her lack of a nurturing instinct toward her children and other family members.

In conclusion, Scarlett's character is based to a very large extent on that of her grandmother, Annie Fitzgerald Stephens, while the relationship between Scarlett and Ellen reflects an attempt by the author to bring closure to her unsettled relationship with her mother, May Belle Stephens Mitchell. Finally, hovering in the background is her pioneer great grandmother, Eleanor McGhan Fitzgerald. The success of *GWTW* is due in large part to the clever layering used by the author to pick and choose elements from the lives of these three women. She stitched them together without ever leaving the slightest trace of a seam.

Chapter 4:
Two Confederate Irish Priests

Fr. Abram J. Ryan

Fr. Abram J. Ryan, the "poet-priest of the Confederacy," as he was called in his day, is mentioned once (730) in the pages of *GWTW*. He is listed among the distinguished visitors who stop by Melanie's humble red brick home on Ivy Street after the war. The fact that his name is mentioned between those of general John B. Gordon, called "Georgia's great hero," and Alex Stephens, the "late Vice-President of the Confederacy," tells us something about the importance that the authorial voice of the novel wants to accord to him.

> Father Ryan, the poet-priest of the Confederacy, never failed to call when passing through Atlanta. He charmed gatherings there with his wit and seldom needed much urging to recite his "Sword of Lee" or his deathless "Conquered Banner," which never failed to make the ladies cry. (730)

Who was Father Ryan, and why did Margaret Mitchell go out of her way to mention him in her novel? He was born on February 5, 1838 in Hagerstown, Maryland, of Irish parents. As a boy he moved west with his parents to St. Louis, where he attended school under the guidance of the Christian Brothers. Sensing that he had a vocation to the priesthood, he entered the seminary in Niagara, New York. After ordination, he returned to the South as a Catholic missionary. When war broke out in 1861, he became a chaplain in the Confederate Army and served the troops in that capacity until the end of the conflict. From this point on, we know a bit more of his life. Stationed first at Nashville, then at Clarksville, Tennessee, he moved on to Augusta, Georgia in about 1867. There he founded the *Banner of the South,* a newspaper which was widely read and quite influential. But in the Reconstruction era, his political views were considered unacceptable to the occupiers, so he had to suspend its publication. At this point, in 1870, he was moved by his bishop to another diocese for political reasons. He thus took up residence in Mobile, Alabama. There he served first as a curate at the Cathedral, establishing a reputation as a preacher. People came from far and wide to hear his sermons, and to relish the verbal fireworks for which he was becoming so well known. Then, in 1877, he was appointed as pastor of St.Mary's Church in that city, a post that he dutifully fulfilled until 1883.

During his thirteen years in Mobile, he continued to devote himself to his literary interests during those free moments that were not consumed by his pastoral duties. It was mostly poems that flowed from his pen, but he also wrote essays and longer prose works. He had been publishing his poems in local newspapers for years, and to this day we do not know how many he actually wrote. But in 1879, the owner of one of the local newspapers, the *Mobile Register,* had the idea of gathering the poems together and printing them in book form. *Father Ryan's Poems* proved to be very successful, and he is said to have earned a substantial sum of money from these efforts, which he then distributed liberally to those in need.

In 1885, having achieved nationwide fame as as a preacher, poet, and writer, he asked his bishop for permission to leave his parochial duties in order to embark on an extended lecture tour around the country. In the course of these travels, he repaired to a Franciscan monastery in Louisville, Kentucky, in the spring of 1886. His intention was to make a retreat there and afterwards to finish his work-in-progress, a *Life of Christ.* It was there that he was called to his eternal reward. He died on April 22, 1886.

Did Fr. Ryan ever meet any members of Margaret Mitchell's extended family? In explaining to one of her admirers, after her initial success in 1936, what it was like growing up in her extended family, Mitchell makes a reference to Father Ryan passing through Atlanta. (see above, page 37) Given the relatively small size of the Irish and Catholic population of Atlanta in the mid-1880's, it is entirely possible that Fr. Ryan could have passed through Atlanta at that time and been present at one such get together. May Belle, who would have been a teenager in 1885, or her mother, might have treasured this experience and passed it on to Margaret. If so, it makes Mitchell's mention of him all the more important. She truly admired the man's work, especially his poem "The Conquered Banner," which school children in the South recited in school for decades, and she did not want it to fall into oblivion. Here is the text of that unforgettable poem.

Furl that Banner, for 'tis weary;
Round its staff 'tis drooping dreary;
     Furl it, fold it, it is best;
For there's not a man to wave it,
And there's not a sword to save it,
And there's not one left to lave it
In the blood which heroes gave it;
And its foes now scorn and brave it;
     Furl it, hide it - let it rest!

***

Take that Banner down! 'tis tattered;
Broken is its staff and shattered;
And the valiant hosts are scattered
     Over whom it floated high.
Oh! 'tis hard for us to fold it;
Hard to think there's none to hold it;
Hard that those who once unrolled it
     Now must furl it with a sigh.

***

Furl that Banner! furl it sadly!
Once ten thousands hailed it gladly,
     And ten thousands wildly, madly,
Swore it should forever wave;
Swore that foeman's sword should never
Hearts like theirs entwined dissever,
Till that flag should float forever
O'er their freedom or their grave!

***

Furl it! for the hands that grasped it,
And the hearts that fondly clasped it,
     Cold and dead are lying low;
And that Banner - it is trailing!
While around it sounds the wailing
     Of its people in their woe.

***

For, though conquered, they adore it!
Love the cold, dead hands that bore it!
Weep for those who fell before it!
Pardon those who trailed and tore it!
But, oh! wildly they deplore it.
     Now who furl and fold it so.

***

Furl that Banner! True 'tis gory,
Yet 'tis wreathed around with glory,
And 'twill live in song and story,
     Though its folds are in the dust:
For its fame on brightest pages,
Penned by poets and by sages,
Shall go sounding down the ages -
     Furl its folds though now we must.

***

Furl that Banner, softly, softly!
Treat it gently - it is holy -
     For it droops above the dead.
Touch it not - unfold it never,
Let it droop there, furled forever.
     For its people's hopes are dead!

It is of interest to note that Fr. Ryan's poem still lives on in countless Civil War monuments throughout the South. Readers of *GWTW* searching for Tara should include in their itinerary visits to the three Confederate monuments in the Atlanta area that evoke the theme. First, the 1910 monument in the Confederate cemetery in Marietta not only depicts Fr. Ryan's "Conquered Banner," it also quotes several verses from the poem. Likewise, the 1908 Confederate monument at the DeKalb County Courthouse in Decatur also reflects the theme of the poem. All four sides of the granite obelisk are devoted to Fr. Ryan's work. Also, hidden away under the magnolias in Atlanta's Oakland Cemetery is the 1894 sculpture of "The Sleeping Lion of the Confederacy." Here, too, the massive head of the slumbering feline is resting on Fr. Ryan's "Conquered Banner." Other such monuments, both in Georgia and throughout the South, also pay homage to the poem in one way or another, often with a quote of a line or two from the poem. It was for this reason that Margaret Mitchell, who was obviously aware of Fr. Ryan's importance, mentions him in her novel. His work, which subsequent generations have unfortunately forgotten, is long overdue for rediscovery.

Fr. Ryan's other famous poem, "The Sword of Robert Lee," is also mentioned in the text of *GWTW*.

> Forth from its scabbard, pure and bright,
> Flashed the sword of Lee!
> Far in the front of the deadly fight,
> High o'er the brave in the cause of Right,
> Its stainless sheen, like a beacon light,
> Led us to Victory.

***

> Out of its scabbard, where, full long,
> It slumbered peacefully,
> Roused from its rest by the battle's song,
> Shielding the feeble, smiting the strong,
> Guarding the right, avenging the wrong,
> Gleamed the sword of Lee.

***

Forth from its scabbard, high in air
Beneath Virginia's sky -
And they who saw it gleaming there,
And knew who bore it, knelt to swear
That where that sword led they would dare
To follow - and to die.

***

Out of its scabbard! Never hand
Waved sword from stain as free,
Nor purer sword led braver band,
Nor braver bled for a brighter land,
Nor brighter land had a cause so grand,
Nor cause a chief like Lee!

***

Forth from its scabbard! How we prayed
That sword might victor be;
And when our triumph was delayed,
And many a heart grew sore afraid,
We still hoped on while gleamed the blade
Of noble Robert Lee.

***

Forth from its scabbard all in vain
Bright flashed the sword of Lee;
'Tis shrouded now in its sheath again,
It sleeps the sleep of our noble slain,
Defeated, yet without a stain,
Proudly and peacefully.

Fr. Thomas O'Reilly

There is another Catholic priest who, because of his important connections to both Atlanta and the Fitzgerald/Stephens family, merits mention here. Fr. Thomas O'Reilly (1831-1872), who baptized May Belle Stephens Mitchell, as well as several other members of the extended Fitzgerald clan, at Immaculate Conception Church, was appointed as pastor of that church in 1861. A native of County Cavan, Ireland, he completed his seminary training at All Hallows Seminary in Dublin, which to this day supplies many priests for the Atlanta Archdiocese. He was ordained in 1857, and took his first missionary assignment shortly thereafter in Savannah. After four years, he moved to Atlanta, and his arrival coincided with the outbreak of war.

During the next three years, he served as a chaplain in the Confederate Army, adding this to his normal pastoral duties. Then, in 1864, as Sherman's army approached, new challenges would emerge. During the summer of that year Sherman mercilessly shelled the civilian population of Atlanta. To many observers, this was a "war crime" if there ever was one. Strangely, however, this term is generally not used to describe Sherman's policies. Is this because he was on the side of the "good guys," that is, the winners of the war who get to write the history books? Then, after the city surrendered in early September, he moved in and set up his military occupation of the town. By early November, Sherman had decided on his next course of action: he would send part of his army north to Tennessee, and he would proceed to Savannah, but not before putting the City of Atlanta to the torch and leaving it a smoldering ruin just as winter was about to set in. This would be yet another "war crime" against the civilian population.

In the meantime, Fr. O'Reilly had been ministering to both Union and Confederate soldiers. Their needs were many: hearing confessions, offering daily Mass, burying the dead with the rites of the Church, writing letters for those who could not do so for themselves, and interceding in so many ways on behalf of those overwhelmed by events. In the course of carrying out his duties, he learned, from Union sources, of Sherman's plan to burn the city to the ground on the night of November 12, 1864. He was outraged about this plan to wage war against the civilian population of the city. He immediately demanded an interview with Sherman, which was not granted. However, through a lower ranking general, he made it clear to Sherman that the wanton destruction of homes and churches was a sin against God's law. But Sherman, a latter-day Cromwell who was full of the hatred that so often inspires those who are convinced of the righteousness of their cause and the diabolical nature of their enemy, was unyielding. So Fr. O'Reilly offered a compromise. Since he could do nothing about Sherman's political decision to devastate the physical wellbeing of the people of Atlanta by destroying their homes just before the onset of cold weather, he could at least show concern for their spiritual wellbeing by sparing their churches. Thus, he asked, or rather threatened, that if Sherman destroyed these churches, all located in the center of the city, he would call upon the many Irish and Catholic soldiers in the Union Army to mutiny. The law of God, he argued, was higher than the law of man, and if any Catholic obeyed a sacrilegious command to destroy a church, he would be excommunicated for his act.

Sherman delayed making his decision for a few days. He didn't like being "threatened" by anybody, least of all an Irish immigrant priest. At the same time he realized how much he depended on the valor of the "Fighting Irish" in the ranks of the Union Army. He wanted to think it over. One option that Sherman considered was to have Fr. O'Reilly executed as a rebel. But that would hardly do, for it wouldn't play well at all in the Northern press. And it might also encourage mutiny in the Union ranks at a critical moment in the Atlanta campaign. Or should he completely ignore the man and call his bluff, torching even the downtown churches? Sherman finally chose the course of compromise. He went ahead, as planned, with his "war crime" against the civilian population, but made sure to spare the downtown area around the churches.

Thus, the five churches that were located at that time in the central city were all saved. They were Immaculate Conception, Trinity Methodist, Central Presbyterian, St Philip's Episcopal and Second Baptist. Since those days, St. Philip's has relocated to Peachtree Street in Buckhead, and Second Baptist to Ponce De Leon Avenue. But the first three are still there, serving the spiritual needs of those who live and work in the central city.

The tourist guides to Atlanta rarely if ever mention the debt owed by the City of Atlanta to this valiant Irish priest. In fact, it took until 1945 for members of the five churches spared in 1864 to get together to erect a monument in his honor. Unfortunately, this small token, which presently sits at the northeast corner of the Atlanta City Hall, is almost completely out of sight.

Fr. O'Reilly died in 1872 at the age of 41. He is buried in the crypt at the Shrine of the Immaculate Conception, as his old parish church is now called. Here, one also finds various memorabilia relating to his life and work. In 1870, his portrait was painted by the well-known Atlanta artist John Maier, and this work is part of the permanent collection of the Atlanta History Center. Unfortunately, like the historical marker near City Hall, few people ever get to see it.

One final question remains. How could Margaret Mitchell *not* have mentioned Fr. O'Reilly in her novel? My answer to this question is that we are not sure that she didn't. Since she had ordered her husband to destroy her notes and manuscripts upon her death, an order that he diligently obeyed, we have no way of knowing what the original drafts of the chapter on the burning of Atlanta looked like. Was Fr. O'Reilly mentioned? In my view, he must have been. But for some reason, when the novel was completed, his name was no longer included.

THE IRISH ROOTS 57

Chapter 5:
Irish History and Song

The Green Irish as Wordsmiths

In our day it is clear that Irish writers are among the greatest literary creators to have ever used the English language to express themselves. There are few if any who would argue with such a statement. But that was not so clear in the 1920's when Mitchell was writing. Nonetheless, she attempted, however discreetly, to celebrate in a number of ways the bardic quality of the Irish druid/priest/orator/poet/storyteller. Most obviously, she hit upon the powerful and mythic word *Tara* to designate her Irish ancestors' plantation home in Clayton County. This was truly a stroke of genius. The word's origins in history and its use by Margaret Mitchell are explored in Chapter 2 of the present study, with particular reference to the poem "The Harp That Once Through Tara's Halls," by the Irish poet Thomas Moore (1779-1852).

But here we can discuss another one of Moore's poems that is specifically cited in *GWTW*, "The Lament for Robert Emmet," also known by the title "She Is Far From the Land Where Her Young Hero Sleeps." (84, 203)

Robert Emmet (1778-1803) had to leave Trinity College, Dublin, in 1798 because of his agitation on behalf of Irish independence. His nationalist sympathies were simply not tolerated. A few years later he played a key role in the unsuccessful nationalist uprising of 1803 in which a group of idealistic young men calling themselves the United Irishmen tried to seize Dublin Castle. Although he escaped from Dublin, he later returned to see his fiancée, Sarah Curran, at which time he was arrested. Convicted of treason against the British Crown, he was hanged by the English on September 20, 1803. He was only 24 years old at the time of his death. Sarah Curran spent the rest of her life in England, where she died in 1808.

Emmet derives his fame from two principal sources: 1) his impassioned speech from the scaffold before his death, and 2) and Moore's poem. The latter stands as an eternal reminder of the sacrifices made through the centuries by so many Irish patriots. Here is the text of Moore's poem.

> She is far from the land where her young hero sleeps,
>   And lovers around her sighing;
> But coldly she turns from their gaze, and weeps,
>   For her heart in the grave is lying.
> She sings the wild songs of her dear native plains,
>   Every note which he loved awaking;
> Ah! little they think, who delight in her strains,
>   How the heart of the minstrel is breaking.

***

> He had lived for his love, for his country he died,
>   They were all that to life had entwined him;
> Nor soon shall the tears of his country be dried,
>   Nor long will his love stay behind him.
> Oh! make her a grave where the sunbeams rest
>   When they promise a glorious morrow;
> They'll shine o'er her sleep, like a smile from the West
>   For her own loved island of sorrow.

Mitchell also commemorates her Green Irish heritage by including in *GWTW* two references (84, 688) to the Irish revolutionary song "The Wearin 'o the Green." It is associated each time with Gerald O'Hara. One of the most famous of all the Irish revolutionary songs, it is a true folk tune, having been created anonymously in 1798 in the streets of Dublin. Here are the words of the original "street version" of the song.

> O Paddy dear, an' did ye hear the news that's goin' round?
> The Shamrock is forbid by law to grow on Irish ground!
> No more St. Patrick's Day we'll keep; his color can't
>   be seen,
> For there's a cruel law agin' the Wearin' o' the Green!

***

Fr. Abram J. Ryan, the "the poet-priest of the Confederacy," in the 1870's.

May Belle Stephens Mitchell in 1904.

Little Peggy, at age 4 in her Celtic armchair.

Fr. Thomas O'Reilly in the 1870's

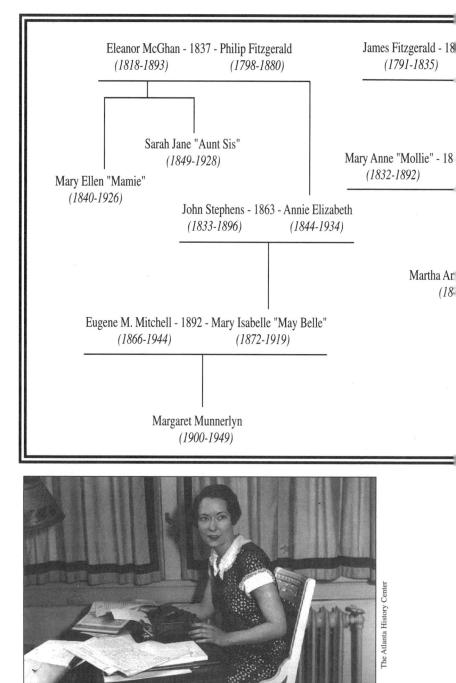

Eleanor McGhan - 1837 - Philip Fitzgerald
(1818-1893) *(1798-1880)*

James Fitzgerald - 18
(1791-1835)

Sarah Jane "Aunt Sis"
(1849-1928)

Mary Anne "Mollie" - 18
(1832-1892)

Mary Ellen "Mamie"
(1840-1926)

John Stephens - 1863 - Annie Elizabeth
(1833-1896) *(1844-1934)*

Martha Ar
(18

Eugene M. Mitchell - 1892 - Mary Isabelle "May Belle"
(1866-1944) *(1872-1919)*

Margaret Munnerlyn
(1900-1949)

The Atlanta History Center

*Is this 1936 photo, Peggy's Remington replaced the harp as the instrument
of choice for the commemoration of her ancestors' "gumption."*

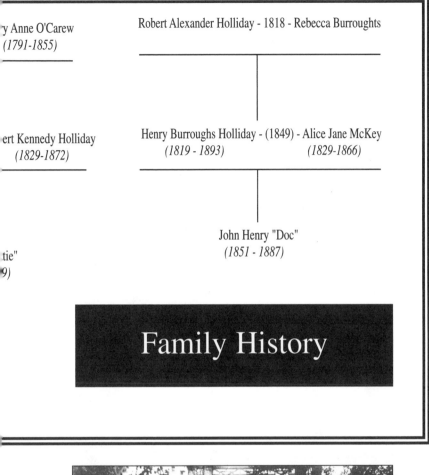

y Anne O'Carew
(1791-1855)

Robert Alexander Holliday - 1818 - Rebecca Burroughts

ert Kennedy Holliday
(1829-1872)

Henry Burroughs Holliday - (1849) - Alice Jane McKey
(1819 - 1893)   *(1829-1866)*

tie"
9)

John Henry "Doc"
(1851 - 1887)

Family History

The Atlanta History Center

*The Mitchells moved into this home at 1401 Peachtree Street in 1912.
Peggy lived here through her formative adolescent years.*

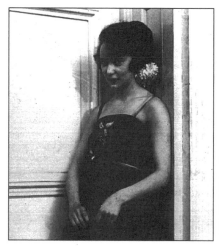

As a deb in 1921, half way between the mystical age of "falling in love" at 16 and the hard work of beginning GWTW at age 26.

The modern woman, cigarette in hand, on a camping trip in 1922.

Another photograph of Peggy as a deb.

With her future husband, "Red" (Rhett) Upshaw, playing the role of Scarlett.

I met with Napper Tandy, and he took me by the hand,
And he said "How's poor old Ireland and how does
    she stand?
She's the most distressful country that ever yet was seen,
They're hangin' men and women for the Wearin' of
    the Green."

***

And if the colour we must wear is England's cruel Red,
Let it remind us of the blood that Ireland has shed;
Then pull the Shamrock from your hat, and throw it on
    the sod,
And never fear, 'twill take root there, tho' under foot
    tis trod.

***

When law can stop the blades of grass from growin' as
    they grow.
And when the leaves in summertime their colors dare
    not show,
Then I will change the color, too, I wear in my caubeen;
But till that day, please God, I'll stick to Wearin' o'
    the Green.

There can be no doubt about Mitchell's intentions in including references to these works in *GWTW*. They were meant to reinforce that particular sense of Irish identity that makes the O'Haras so real and so believable, as well as to reflect the depth of her own Irish roots.

The Orange Irish as Wordsmiths

The Catholics, or Green Irish, and the Protestants, or Orange Irish, have been at war for centuries. Since the days in the seventeenth century when England imported Scotch Presbyterians into Ulster, the northernmost of Ireland's provinces, in order the dilute the Irish and Catholic population, there has been continuous religious strife. Margaret Mitchell was very conscious of this cleavage in Irish society. She had heard her Fitzgerald relatives speak of it many times, so it was only natural for her to include it in her novel. In fact, since her father's heritage was Scottish and Protestant, Mitchell had lived with these competing visions from infancy.

Gerald O'Hara is a refugee from the "troubles" in Ireland. In fact he would not have come to this country if he had not killed the rent collector sent by his absentee landlord. When Gerald had called him "a bastard of an Orangeman," (44) the man retorted by "whistling the opening bars of 'The Boyne Water.'" (45) In *GWTW*, the term "Orangeman" is used four times (44, 51, 203, 694) and refers not only to Protestants from Ulster, but also to people in this country, like Rhett Butler, who sympathize with their point of view.

The term originated as a reference to supporters of King William III, of the House of Orange, and his victory over the Catholic King James II, at the battle of the Boyne, near the town of Drogheda, on July 12, 1690. (45) A century later, Orangemen's Day was established in Ulster in 1795 as a way of resisting the growing groundswell of agitation for emancipation of Catholics. To this day, the descendants of the Orangemen commemorate this victory in a rather bizarre manner. Revelers, wearing orange sashes or orange-colored flowers in their lapels, parade through the Catholic neighborhoods of Belfast, taunting the descendants of those who were defeated at the Boyne. In this country, Orangemen's Day was celebrated widely through the 1930's.

The principal representative of the Orangemen in *GWTW* is Angus MacIntosh, Gerald O'Hara's neighbor. He lives with his family in his plantation home which is located about a mile from Tara. (51) In the social pecking order in the County, they rank ahead of the Slattery family, but below the rest of the gentry. Since this family is of Scotch-Irish origin, and originally came from Ulster, (51) they are anathema to Gerald O'Hara, and the O'Hara family looks down on them. Scarlett has inherited from her father strong feelings of dislike for this family. For example, when she tries to think up new ways to insult Rhett, she tries to think of "things she had heard Gerald call Mr. Lincoln, the MacIntoshes and balky mules..." (384).

The MacIntosh plantation home is burned to the ground in 1864, (392) but they are able to obtain compensation later from the Federal government when they agree to take the Iron Clad Oath and state that they had never accepted the legality of the Confederacy. (691) In this they are once again at odds with the O'Hara family who, like Mitchell's Fitzgerald and Stephens ancestors, are staunch Confederates.

"The Boyne Water," still sung to this day by the Orangemen as they march through the Catholic neighborhoods of Belfast each year, celebrates the Protestant victory of 1690. Here are a few selected stanzas of the song. (45)

> July the First, of a morning clear, one thousand
>   six hundred and ninety,
> King William did his men prepare, of thousands he
>   had thirty;
> To fight King James and all his foes, encamped near
>   the Boyne Water,
> He little fear'd, though two to one, their multitudes
>   to scatter.

***

> King William call'd his officers, saying: "Gentlemen,
>   mind your station,
> And let your valor here be shown before this
>   Irish nation;
> My brazen walls let no man break, and your subtle
>   foes you'll scatter,
> Be sure you show them good English play as you go over
> the water."

***

> Both foot and horse they marched on, intending them
>   to batter,
> But the brave Duke Schomberg he was shot as he cross'd
>   over the water.
> When that King William did observe the brave Duke
>   Schomberg falling,

He rein'd his horse with a heavy heart, on the
    Enniskilleners calling:

***

"What will you do for me, brave boys - see yonder men
    retreating?
Our enemies encourag'd are and English drums are
    beating;"
He says: "My boys, feel no dismay at the losing of
    one commander,
For God shall be our king this day, and I'll be
    general under."

***

Within four yards of our fore-front, before a shot
    was fired,
A sudden snuff they got that day, which little
    they desired;
For horse and man fell to the ground, and some hung
    in their saddle:
Others turn'd up their forked ends, which we call
    'coup de ladle.'

***

Prince Eugene's regiment was the next, on our right
    hand advanced,
Into a field of standing wheat, where Irish horses pranced -
But the brandy ran so in their heads, their senses all
    did scatter,
They little thought to leave their bones that day at
    the Boyne Water.

***

Both men and horse lay on the ground, and many
    there lay bleeding:
I saw no sickles there that day - but, sure, there was
    sharp shearing.

***

Now, praise God, all true Protestants, and heaven's
and earth's Creator,
For the deliverance that he sent our enemies to scatter.
The Church's foes will pine away, like churlish-hearted
Nabal,
For our deliverer came this day like the great Zorobabel.

***

So praise God, all true Protestants, and I will say no
further,
But had the Papists gain'd the day there would have
been open murder.
Although King James and many more were ne'er
that way inclined,
It was not in their power to stop what the rabble
they designed.

Other References to Irish History in *GWTW*.

Mitchell also includes in *GWTW* a number of passing references to various historical figures and events from Irish history.
These references are not a mere filler for the novel, but serve to
reinforce the Irish framework that envelops Scarlett and her
family. It is part of the work's delicate scaffolding. These references provide background for the major characters and help to
bring them to life on the page.

I shall mention the three principal ones here: the Banshees,
Brian Boru, and Oliver Cromwell/Drogheda.

In Irish and Gaelic folklore, the Banshee (271) is the female
spirit who warns a family of approaching death. She does this
either by her appearance or, especially, by wailing unseen under
the windows of the house a night or two before the time of the
death she foretells.

Mitchell also invokes the name of Brian Boru (940-1014?),
the ancient King of Ireland, (92) who of course is referred to by
Gerald O'Hara. The head of a major clan in the province of

Munster in the south of Ireland, Brian Boru eventually became high king of all of Ireland. Unfortunately, his power was challenged by the Norsemen who ruled the coasts of that country. The final battle in the struggle between Brian Boru and the Norse occurred on Good Friday, April 23, 1014 at Clontarf, not far from the town of Drogheda. Although victorious against the foreign invader, Brian Boru was later slain in his tent by dissidents from his own army.

Oliver Cromwell (1599-1658) was the military, political and religious leader of England, and Lord Protector of the Commonwealth (1653-1658), who played a dominant role during a time of exceptional turmoil in English history. His victory over the Irish Catholics at the Battle of Drogheda in 1649 had a devastating effect on the Irish people. Those thousands of Irish who were not deported to the West Indies as white slaves, would remain enslaved in their own country for centuries under English oppression. There is a discernible pattern in these three references, each of which tells of death and defeat. The Irish are attacked, indeed invaded by a conquering aggressor, the English, who seek to impose their will upon the Irish people, going so far as to strip them of their national identity, customs and language. It is not difficult to see the connection between these references to Irish history and the general tendency of *GWTW* to paint the Yankees as aggressors and the Southerners as victims of their aggression. There is thus a deep complicity in the text of *GWTW* between the Irish and the Confederates as victims of arrogant and well-armed aggressors. This is another reason why so many academic liberals dislike *GWTW*. They know that the ongoing rape of Ireland by England cannot be justified, and they hate to see this crime equated with what the North did to the South in the Civil War.

In *GWTW*, this background of persecution of the Irish race also helps to raise Scarlett's obsession with saving Tara from a merely anecdotal to an epic level of meaning. The novel implies that the Irish people, no matter where they live, must always be on their guard, and until their homeland is completely free and independent, they will always be at the mercy of such forces. Scarlett thus takes her place alongside the victims of Cromwell at Drogheda, and the ancient king Brian Boru. She is an exemplar of the race and its desire to survive against all odds.

Finally, the Irish also figure in *GWTW* as one of the major (145, 649) European immigrant groups which, with the Germans, were heavily recruited into the Union Army during the Civil War. Gerald O'Hara wonders why they can't see that in fighting for the Union they are going against their own best interests. This situation causes him no end of anxiety. Thus, by 1862, he is fed up with "the blackguardery of the Irish who were being enticed into the Yankee army by bounty money." (202) In this regard, Ashley also laments that the Yankees are recruiting "wild Irishmen who talk Gaelic." (272) A house divided against itself might survive, but it cannot prosper.

Chapter 6:
The Irish and Blacks as House Servants

"Bridget," the Irish Maid

Margaret Mitchell is among the most observant of American writers when it comes to social nuances. But in addition to her powers of observation, she also has the ability to dramatize the lessons drawn from those observations. There is perhaps no better example of these powers at work in *GWTW* than when she compares and contrasts Northern and Southern preferences for house servants.

This subject is developed in the larger context of the Irish and hard work, a theme to which Mitchell seems to return again and again. Thus she goes out of her way to include that permanent fixture of polite society in 19th century America: "Bridget," or "Biddie," the Irish maid. Every nice family had one. But Mitchell treats the subject with a clever twist.

When Scarlett is approached by the wife of a Yankee officer from Maine, the lady tells her that she is in search of an Irish nurse to take care of her children, her "Bridget" having fled back to the North because she cannot "stay another day down here among the 'naygurs' as she calls them." (663) Why is this Yankee lady associated with Maine? Could it be because that state is as far to the north as any state can be, and had to be among the states with the smallest number of negroes in the 1860's? The initial image of the Irish that is projected by the Yankee lady's words is negative. But of course it is not "Bridget" who is speaking for herself. Rather, it is her mistress who is putting words in her mouth. Thus, not only are the Irish of the servant class, they also express prejudice against black folks. How dreadful for a Yankee lady to have to endure such low class people! So Scarlett naturally - and logically - recommends to this socially enlightened woman that she "find a darky girl just in from the country who hasn't been spoiled by the Freedmen's Bureau." As usual, Scarlett is being blunt, but honest. She is talking like her model, Annie Fitzgerald Stephens, Margaret Mitchell's grandmother. But then the tables are completely turned when the lady from Maine explodes: "Do you think I'd trust my babies to a black nigger? I want a good Irish girl." At which point Scarlett reminds her that since there are "no Irish servants in Atlanta," she should look for a black woman. "I assure you that darkies aren't cannibals and are quite trustworthy." (663) The denouement to this most interesting scene is quite unexpected, for Mitchell has led us onto a subject that the reader is not quite ready for at this point. The scene also raises a number of questions about the hypocrisy of the lady in question, the forerunner of a certain type of white liberal that is still with us today.

In this scene, Mitchell kills several birds with one stone. First of all, she puts the accusation of supposed Irish prejudice against black folks in perspective, reminding us that, if it does indeed exist, the same prejudice also exists among the social elites. The only difference is that the latter have more subtle means - at least on the surface - of expressing it. Then, as now, they are ready to ascribe feelings of prejudice to lower class whites, while seeing themselves as beacons of enlightenment.

The second point that Mitchell makes concerns the paradoxical relations between blacks and whites in the South in the 19th century. Although the political rights of black people were severely limited by law, blacks and whites often lived their whole lives together in the same house. As a result, many of them came to know each other extremely well, with feelings of affection and esteem often outweighing the master/servant basis of their relationship. There was a closeness between them as people that was truly remarkable. Ironically, it was perhaps fostered by the very legal system that was designed to keep them separate!

Of course, the reason why Mitchell creates this scene in the first place is to get these ideas across to her readers. Not surprisingly, there are a number of important connections between Scarlett and the Yankee lady from Maine on the one hand, and Margaret Mitchell's family, on the other. I will touch on two of them later in the chapter.

Finally, where did Mitchell get her ideas about the special obligation that whites, especially those in positions of power, have toward blacks? As Marianne Walker reminds us in her biography of Mitchell, *Margaret Mitchell & John Marsh: The Love Story Behind* **Gone With the Wind**, it was from her mother that Mitchell derived her concerns about equal rights for blacks: "Maybelle was also more sensitive about everything than Eugene [her husband] was. She was concerned about the poor and the injustices heaped upon women and blacks - injustices that do not seem to have bothered Eugene at all."[17]

This lesson about the special obligations toward blacks is reflected in the unforgettable scenes from *GWTW* in which Scarlett attempts to entice the former household servants to work in the fields. One day, Prissy, who in my view suffers from undiagnosed learning disabilities, causes Scarlett to lose her temper. She blurts out: "You're a fool nigger and the worst day's work Pa ever did was to buy you..." (394) Then she realizes what she has done. "There, she thought, I've said the word 'nigger' and Mother wouldn't like that at all." (394) A few days later, she goes after Pork in the same way, "dispensing with the usual forms of courtesy her mother had always taught her to use with negroes." (416) Each time that Scarlett does this, she realizes immediately that she has transgressed her mother's moral code. Thus, the lesson of *GWTW* is clear. At the heart of the novel, the authorial voice preaches the need for kindness, courtesy and respect, without which the races will not be able to get along. May Belle Mitchell's ideas on these matters are put directly into the novel.

Grace, the Former Fitzgerald Slave, and Mammy

In the Fayetteville City Cemetery, where Margaret Mitchell's Fitzgerald ancestors are buried, there is a headstone that reads: "Grace, colored servant of Fitzgeralds." How is this to be explained, especially since blacks and whites, servants and masters, were traditionally buried apart from each other? Who, in other words, was Grace? According to Fitzgerald family lore, Grace belonged to one of the old planters of the area. When he died, his estate was to be divided and Grace did not know what would become of her. She was old and unwanted, and feared that she would be sold to an uncaring family. Even worse, she would risk being separated from relatives living in

17. Atlanta: Peachtree Publishers, 1993. p. 33

Clayton County. She begged James Fitzgerald, the brother of Margaret Mitchell's great grandfather, Philip Fitzgerald, to purchase her. James had become widely respected in the community, despite people's initial fear of his Catholicism and his thick Irish brogue. Although a man of means who could afford to own slaves, he chose not to. But when confronted by this unusual request, he complied with Grace's wishes and purchased her. Grace was so grateful to him for this gesture that she made yet another special and rather unique request: to be buried, after her death, at her master's feet. The Fitzgerald family carried out this request, thereby enabling Grace to express her gratitude.

We cannot talk of Grace from the Fitzgerald household without saying a few words about *GWTW*'s Mammy, who is one of the most unforgettable characters in American fiction. Her sympathetic portrayal by Margaret Mitchell in *GWTW* underscores how close some whites and blacks could become in both the antebellum and the pre-Civil Rights South.

Mammy's interaction with Ellen, on the one hand, and with Scarlett on the other, illustrates the parallel lives lived by negro and white folks within the same household under the slavery system. Mammy, after all, had been raised in Ellen's mother's bedroom so that "her code of conduct and her sense of pride were as high or higher than those of her owners." (25) Although Mammy is black, she has internalized the white value system and enforces it with other whites like Scarlett.

The principal element of enforcement of separateness between the races is not so much color as language. Since slaves are not allowed to learn to read, they have no way of knowing how the words that they pronounce are related to any objective, written code. Language thus remains a function of color. One speaks in the idiom that is appropriate to one's color. Thus, despite the fact that Mammy is extremely intelligent and iron-willed, she remains a slave primarily through language. If she were ever emancipated and wanted to change her social situation, a first step would be to learn to speak differently.

Mammy, as a slave, cannot be officially consulted by her mistress on any matter that does not directly impinge upon her household responsibilities, nor can she express her opinion about family matters that are none of her business. Despite these official boundaries and limits, Mammy seldom hesitates to let her thoughts and feelings be known. She usually does this by mumbling under her breath, and this grumbling almost always takes place while she is in motion, walking from one place to another, usually away from the person, Ellen, to whom her speech is directed. Thus, Ellen is aware of Mammy's opinion on all important matters without having asked for it or having heard it expressed directly!

All these precautionary measures are necessary to avoid seeming to overstep the bounds that separate the slave from her mistress. But these bounds are nonetheless overstepped when Mammy feels a need to express what she thinks. A good example of this occurs after Ellen spends a night tending to a girl from the Slattery family who is in labor. Mammy disapproves of this act of charity on the grounds that the Slattery family is poor white trash. Ellen should not expend her precious energies on *them*, and Mammy lets her know what she thinks by using the indirect method described above. Of course, Ellen hears every word that Mammy says, but, true to the code, makes believe she does not hear and, of course, does not respond. But the important thing is that Mammy has had her say.

Later, during the war, while Scarlett is living on Peachtree Street in Atlanta, Ellen falls sick nursing these same poor white folks and this illness leads to her death. When Mammy sees Scarlett again, she has no trouble expressing her thoughts on this matter. She derides the Slatterys, and there is both understanding and agreement between Mammy and Scarlett on this matter. It is almost as if race is not a factor in their relationship. Similarly, when Scarlett in 1866 decides to make a dress out of a drape in order to look her best as she sets out to find the money to pay the taxes on Tara, no words need be spoken to Mammy. She understands why Scarlett is going to Atlanta. Through her silence, she gives her consent to Scarlett's plan, but by this time Mammy has assumed the role of surrogate mother for Scarlett, and they see eye to eye on the need to preserve their traditional way of life.

In summary, Mammy's relationship to the O'Hara family, with its many built-in safety valves and channels of communication, was deliberately created by Mitchell as an alternative way of looking at the Old South. She despised Harriet Beecher Stowe's one-dimensional *Uncle Tom's Cabin*,[18] which she saw

---

18. Harriet Beecher Stowe (1811-1896) published her first novel, *Uncle Tom's Cabin*, as a serialized novel, beginning in 1851 in the *National Era* magazine. It had tremendous influence both in the North and in Europe, where Stowe toured triumphantly in 1853, 1856 and 1859. In this work, the Southern whites are completely evil, and there is nothing in the slavery system to alleviate the conditions of Negro servitude.

as just another example of Yankee hypocrisy, and she wanted to counter it in *GWTW*. Thus, in creating Mammy, who is so intelligent and strong-willed, yet happy in her day-to-day existence (and whose life is paralleled by Uncle Peter in the Hamilton family), Mitchell was trying to make a political point. Although a slave, Mammy in many ways is the true mistress of the O'Hara household.

Margaret Mitchell's Negro Servants

The theme of kindness and respect found in the pages of *GWTW* is also reflected in the reality of Margaret Mitchell's adult life. Bessie Jordan, her maid, and Carrie Holbrook, her laundress, worked in her household for over twenty years, and Mitchell was very attached to both of them. Although Mitchell was adamant about protecting her private life, even when it involved generosity to her servants, we are still able to piece together the essentials of the relationship between Margaret and her husband on the one hand, and the Jordans on the other. In letters to the *Atlanta Constitution* in 1936 and again in 1951, as well as in a number of other ways, Bessie spelled out in some detail the nature of her mistress's generosity. Although Mitchell biographer Darden Pyron tells us that Bessie Jordan and Mitchell had an "archaic relationship," he still has to concede that the bond between the two women was "real and powerful for both parties during Mitchell's lifetime."[19]

As for Carrie Holbrook, Mitchell's laundress, who died of cancer, she escapes Pyron's notice, but Anne Edwards has a few words to say about her, and they touch upon the subject at hand. According to Edwards, as Carrie was dying, her family, "who were proud people....tried to find a noncharitable hospital bed in which Carrie could die more comfortably than at home." She goes on:

> Peggy tried every paying hospital in the Atlanta area, but none of them would take Carrie. Finally, Peggy threw herself upon the sisters of Our Lady of Perpetual Help, and begged them to violate their rule that patients should be friendless and without family. Carrie was taken in and a "donation" was arranged. Three days later, she died.[20]

19. See Pyron's *Southern Daughter* for a discussion of this relationship. (416)
20. See her *Road to Tara*, p. 321.

Some might call such an action by Mitchell on behalf of her laundress another example of an "archaic relationship," but to me it smacks of plain, old-fashioned kindness.

New depth has been given to this story in the last few years as more information about Mitchell's private life has been unearthed. According to Don O'Briant,[21] Mitchell exchanged more than fifty letters with Dr. Benjamin Mays, who was President of Morehouse College in the late 1940's. Furthermore, it was she who crossed the social divide by initiating the contact because of her desire to finance scholarships for black medical students. Her only stipulation was that this be done quietly and out of the limelight. Such was her way, as we know, but in a matter like this, in the era of segregation, she was also no doubt trying to protect her conservative family from establishment criticism. According to Don O'Briant, "Mitchell's motivation to improve medical care for blacks was fueled in part by the white medical establishment's cruel treatment of her maid. Carrie Holbrook was dying of cancer, and despite Mitchell's pleas, no white hospital would admit her. Mitchell wrote in subsequent letters to Mays that her donations were given in Holbrook's memory."

Other details about Mitchell's generosity have begun to leak out. Dr. Otis Smith, one of the twenty or so young men whose medical education at Morehouse was financed by Margaret Mitchell's anonymous generosity, always wondered who had provided the funds that made his career possible, and now he knows. Dr. Smith, who serves as the Vice Chairman of Margaret Mitchell House, Inc., would like to locate the other doctors who were assisted by Mitchell. "We want to bring them to Atlanta and talk about the impact Margaret Mitchell had on our lives. It would be dynamite to offer a program to high school students....where these doctors could share their experience and inspire others."

Thus, the page devoted to Irish and black house servants in *GWTW* does not appear there by accident. It was written out of Mitchell's deep convictions about respect for others and her sense of *noblesse oblige*. She was convinced that those who serve are not diminished thereby, and can still be people of substance, character and moral worth. Conversely, those who have been blessed with financial wealth in this life bear a grave

---

21. Don O'Briant, "The Mitchell Connection," *The Atlanta Constitution*, March 29, 1995. O'Briant alludes in this article to an untitled work in progress by Ira Joe Johnson.

responsibility to be just and generous to those who work for them. The narrative voice of *GWTW* says damaging things from time to time about both black and Irish people. Yet both groups had a special place in Margaret Mitchell's heart.

Part II
The Catholic Roots

Chapter 7:
Melanie and Her Model, a Catholic Nun

Martha Anne Holliday

First-time readers of *GWTW* usually wonder who might have been the model for the character of Melanie. She is so good, so determined to always see Scarlett in the best light, despite whatever suspicions she might have about her sister-in-law's designs on her husband, and so loving! But at the same time, this lovely, gracious and unassuming woman is also such a determined Confederate! And what courage! Scarlett, after having killed the Union soldier who intrudes upon Tara, "saw in a flash of clarity untouched by any petty emotion that beneath the gentle voice and the dovelike eyes of Melanie there was a thin flashing blade of unbreakable steel, felt too that there were banners and bugles in Melanie's quiet blood." (434) What other character in *GWTW* is more devoted, with all the strength of her being, to the Confederate Cause?

Without a doubt, Martha Anne Holliday (1849-1939), called "Mattie" Holliday, the cousin of Margaret Mitchell's mother, is the major inspiration for the character of Melanie. Mitchell herself made no secret of this.

Mattie's mother, Mary Anne Fitzgerald Holliday, was the daughter of James Fitzgerald, the older brother of Philip Fitzgerald (1798-1880), Margaret Mitchell's great grandfather. (We recall from Chapter 6 that it was James Fitzgerald who bought the slave Grace at the latter's request.) Thus, Mary Anne Fitzgerald was the first cousin of Annie Fitzgerald Stephens (1844-1934), Margaret Mitchell's grandmother. This makes Mattie Holliday the first cousin, once removed, of Margaret Mitchell's mother, May Belle Stephens Mitchell (1872-1919).

Mary Anne Fitzgerald married Robert Holliday in Fayette County on June 16, 1848, and Mattie, the first of eight children, was born a year later, on December 14, 1849. The records of Immaculate Conception Church in Atlanta indicate that Robert Holliday converted to Catholicism at some point prior to the birth of his oldest child. Thus, all of his offspring were baptized and raised as Catholics. Likewise, Annie Fitzgerald married John Stephens in Immaculate Conception Church some time during the summer of 1863. Their daughter, Mary Isabelle, or May Belle, would become the mother of Margaret Mitchell. Although Mattie was twenty-three years older than May Belle, they considered themselves to be cousins, which was perfectly normal in the context of the extended Southern family as it existed in those days. Another reason for this feeling of closeness was that Mattie Holliday saw so much of Annie Fitzgerald, and later of her daughter. They grew up near each other in Jonesboro, and later lived around the corner from each other on Jackson Street in Atlanta.

According to Victoria Wilcox, Chairman of The Holliday House Association, Inc., in Fayette County, Mattie's father, Robert Holliday (1829-1872), was a noted businessman, first in Fayetteville, where he lived from 1848 until 1854, and then in Jonesboro, where he lived from 1854 until his death in 1872. There he owned a mercantile and business building on Main Street facing the railroad, as well as several other pieces of property, and also served as a school board member and county clerk. With the advent of war in 1861, he was commissioned directly into the Confederate Army with the rank of captain in the Quartermaster Corps. He remained in that position throughout the war with his principal responsibilities being the care of the sick and wounded, and the provision of food and other supplies to the troops. This aspect of his experience during the war reminds us of the character Frank Kennedy, also a man of means, who serves in the Confederate Commissary doing basically what Mattie's father had done. It should be noted, however, that Robert Holliday did not spend the whole war in Atlanta. On the contrary, he was out campaigning most of the time. For example, during 1863, he served with the 7th Georgia Regiment of Anderson's Brigade, Hood's Division, Longstreet's Corps at Gettysburg. While on a foraging expedition in the spring of 1864, from Virginia into North Carolina, Captain Holliday's wagon train was captured by Union forces and he was taken prisoner. At the end of the war he signed the Oath of Allegiance at Raleigh and was released. But it took him many weeks to walk back home to Georgia, and he didn't rejoin his family until some time during the summer of 1865. Mattie blamed his premature death seven years later, at the age of 44 leaving eight young children, on his trials during the Civil War, but especially on the cruel treatment that he received in a Yankee prison camp. While he was serving in the Army, his family remained in Jonesboro. He came back to Atlanta on furlough in February, 1864, at which time he took his oldest daughter, Mattie, and one of her sisters, to Savannah, in order to shelter them from the effects of the war. General Sherman was just then leaving Tennessee and making his way toward Atlanta. Holliday enrolled his daughters at St. Vincent's Academy where they remained until December, 1864.

Meanwhile, Mattie's mother, Mary Anne Fitzgerald Holliday, at the urging of her uncle, Philip Fitzgerald, left Atlanta in August, 1864, and travelled to his farm, which was located about 4 miles outside of Jonesboro. They left because elements of Sherman's army were preparing to attack the town. In retrospect, they were well advised to do so, since the Holliday buildings were burned to the ground by Sherman's forces after they swept through the town on August 31 - September 1, 1864.

After staying at the Fitzgerald farm outside Jonesboro for two weeks, they continued their journey farther toward the south. Their destination was Valdosta, where Robert Holliday's brother, Henry Burroughs Holliday (1819-1893), whose only son was John Henry, the future "Doc" Holliday, had acquired a farm some seven miles outside of town. He and his family were also refugeeing from the town of Griffin, where John Henry had been born and grew up. They too were going south to escape the Union Army. Mattie and her sister came from Savannah to join their relatives in December, 1864. The Hollidays stayed in Valdosta until Robert Holliday's return from the war in the summer of 1865, at which time they returned to Griffin and Jonesboro.

It was during these months of living together that Mattie, now about sixteen years old, had an extended period of time in which to get to know her first cousin, John Henry, who was nineteen months her junior (born August 14, 1851). But even after the war, the two families continued to visit back and forth between Jonesboro and Griffin, so that there were further contacts between the two young people. Another lengthy stay together occurred in the summer of 1867 or 1868, when John

Henry became involved in what was probably a shooting incident near home. His family sent him to Jonesboro for an extended visit while things simmered down in Griffin. At this time, John Henry was a handsome and hot-blooded boy of 16, and Mattie a petite and attractive lass of 17 and a half years old. In addition, Mattie was already 2 years older than her own mother had been when she married. That must have been an interesting summer.

John Henry was bent on obtaining an education, intending to become a dentist. He studied two sessions (March-September 1870-71 and 1871-72) at the Pennsylvania College of Dental Surgery in Philadelphia, and graduated in March, 1872. Since he could not practice legally in Georgia until he was 21, he worked in St. Louis for a while, and then came to Atlanta in July, 1872. Upon his 21st birthday, he received his inheritance, which included a commercial building in Griffin. He seems to have practiced dentistry there for some time until leaving Georgia for good in September, 1873. His destination was Texas, where he practiced with a prominent partner in Dallas until they split in March, 1874. Soon John Henry would be arrested for the first of eight times in Texas, all but one for gambling. Mattie must have known that he would have a hard time without her steadying influence in his life, which is why she kept up such a devoted correspondence with him. In this connection, a reader of *GWTW* cannot help but think of Philippe Robillard, Ellen's cousin, who also gets into trouble when he goes out west, and is killed in a brawl. Perhaps even more reminiscent of John Henry Holliday, is the character of Tony Fontaine. After he gets into trouble in Georgia, he, like "Doc," runs off to Texas to start a new life.

Through the years, some members of the Holliday and Fitzgerald families came to suppose that Mattie and John Henry "fell in love" with each other. According to this theory, such a love was doomed from the outset because there was no possibility of anything ever materializing from this relationship, the principal impediment being Mattie's Catholic faith. Georgia law at the time allowed first cousins to marry, and it had happened before in the Holliday family. But marriage between first cousins was forbidden by the canon law of the Catholic Church. Also, John Henry, who was baptized a Presbyterian and later became a Methodist when his mother embraced that faith, could not have married Mattie even if he converted to Catholicism. It still would not have done any good, for canon law forbade a marriage between first cousins. The alternative, a marriage outside the Church, which was of course a possibility under Georgia law, would not be recognized by the Church. If Mattie were to do this, she would be living in sin.

We cannot know for sure what this supposed "falling in love" meant to each of them, and we can only guess at the means they used to express their feelings. It is certain that they were attracted to each other, but this attraction most likely took place on a purely spiritual plane. The mutual respect and affection that they had for each other is reflected in the fact that she was the only member of his large and extended family with whom John Henry ever bothered to maintain contact after he began his wanderings around at least a half dozen states after the end of the Civil War. They corresponded for many years, and relatives of Sister Mary Melanie have quoted her as saying that if she had not destroyed his many letters, the image that has been passed down to us of "Doc" Holliday as a reckless gambler and gunslinger would be quite different today.

Mattie received her high school certificate from Clayton High School in Jonesboro in 1867 when she was eighteen years of age. We cannot be sure if she had a desire to enter a convent at this time, or if the call to religious life came later. In any case, it would have been difficult to enter a convent in the years following the Civil War, for there was simply no room for any more sisters in the existing convents in the South. In the wake of that conflict, there were so many women who wanted to enter religious life that the demand could not be accommodated. And Mattie, who in later years never hid her dislike of the Yankees for what they had done to the South, the South for her being Jonesboro and Georgia, would not consider entering a convent in the North! Thus, she waited many years for an opening and finally began her life as a nun when she entered Saint Vincent's Convent in Savannah on October 1, 1883. She became a postulant in the Sisters of Mercy and took the religious name of Sister Mary Melanie. She would remain a healthy and active member of the order for the next 56 years, until her death on April 9, 1939.

For most of her years as a nun she was a teacher, first in Savannah, then in Augusta, where she served as Sister Superior at Sacred Heart Convent. Later she was sent to Atlanta, where she worked as the cashier at Saint Joseph's Infirmary and later lived at Immaculate Conception Convent on Washington Street in downtown Atlanta. It was in her later years, while in semi-retirement at St.Joseph's Infirmary, later St. Joseph's Hospital, that she would make a daily visit to the bedside of Margaret Mitchell's husband, John Marsh, when he was sick in late 1936 and early 1937. Anne Edwards quotes a nurse who cared for Marsh at this time as saying that "there was a nun who was quite old. She was a cousin [of Peggy's] - second or third - named Sister Melanie. Mrs. Marsh would stop in to see her. She told me that was where the name 'Melanie' came from." (259)

In addition to this revelation, which only came about after the novel was published, and purely by accident, there are also two clues in the text of *GWTW* about the relationship between Melanie and Mattie Holliday. The first is that Melanie excels at raising chickens, which was also one of Sister Melanie's interests for many years as a nun. Thus, when Scarlett returns to Tara for Gerald's funeral, one of the first things that Will Benteen tells her is that "Miss Melly's done mighty well with the hens, yes sir, she has. She's a fine woman." (689) The other clue has to do with the physical description of Melanie in the novel. It bears an amazing resemblance to a photo of Mattie Holliday taken when she was a girl. It is almost as if Mitchell had the picture in front of her when she penned the description of Melanie's face.[22]

> She was a tiny, frailly built girl, who gave the appearance of a child masquerading in her mother's enormous hoop skirts - an illusion that was heightened by the shy, almost frightened look in her too large brown eyes. She had a cloud of curly dark hair which was so sternly repressed beneath its net that no vagrant tendrils escaped, and this dark mass, with its long widow's peak, accentuated the heart shape of her face. Too wide across the cheek bones, too pointed at the chin, it was a sweet, timid face but a plain face, and she had no feminine tricks

22. This picture was published in *The Atlanta Constitution* on Sunday, July 3, 1994, in a big spread on the first page of the Living section.

of allure to make observers forget its plainness.
She looked - and was - as simple as the earth,
as good as bread, as transparent as spring
water. But for all her plainness of feature and
smallness of stature, there was a sedate dignity
about her movements that was oddly touching
and far older than her seventeen years. (103-4)

Finally, yet another reflection of the deep affection that existed between Sister Mary Melanie and her cousin is the fact that "Doc" Holliday converted to Catholicism. This might have occurred as early as 1872, about fifteen years before his death. He did not have to convert, but must have done so because of his cousin's influence. In fact, his obituary in *The Denver Republican* mentions a cousin who had a benign influence on him and who was a "Sister of Charity." Although Sister Mary Melanie was actually a Sister of Mercy, the two orders were related. But, perhaps more importantly, Sister Melanie was known to "Doc" as well as to all who knew her as a true "sister of charity."[23]

Mattie Holliday Transposed in *GWTW*

As we have already seen, Margaret Mitchell drew deeply on family lore in writing her great novel. In fact, at the heart of *GWTW*, we find Mattie Holliday, or Sister Mary Melanie, ranking right beside the inspiration provided by Mitchell's mother, grandmother and great grandmother. The fact that Mitchell gave the name of Melanie to one of the major characters of *GWTW* is a testimony to the life of self-sacrifice that her cousin had lived.

Mitchell does this in an ingenious way. She takes the oral accounts of Mattie's life that had been passed down to her, and focusses her attention on the crisis that might have taken place in Mattie's life when she was a girl of sixteen. This becomes the mighty theme of "impossible love" that echoes from one end of *GWTW* to the other, with variations on it woven throughout the text. Imagining Mattie, a teenager, as being in love with a man whom she could not marry because of impediments that are beyond her control, she develops three variations on this theme,

---

23. I lean heavily in this section on the Holliday family historians. See Albert S. Pendleton, Jr., and Susan McKey Thomas, *In Search of the Hollidays: the Story of Doc Holliday and His Holliday and McKey families.* Valdosta, GA: Little River Press, 105 East Moore Street, 1973.

one major and two minor.

The principal one, which is the case of Scarlett, is at the heart of the novel. Scarlett cannot marry Ashley for the simple reason that he is married to Melanie, herself a reflection of Mattie!

But what about the two minor variations on the theme? The first has to do with Ellen Robillard. As a girl of about sixteen, she is forbidden to marry her first cousin, Philippe, for reasons that remain shrouded in mystery. The family also forces him to leave Charleston and move to New Orleans. When she learns later that he has been killed in a brawl in that city, she is tempted to enter a convent, but is forbidden to do so by her father. Thus, her first and natural outlet, to enter religious life as a form of penance for having been too much in love with the pleasures and lures of the world, is denied. This explains why she agrees to marry Gerald O'Hara, the blustery little man who is twice her age and, as an uneducated immigrant, her social inferior. She enters marriage as a kind of penance.

The second minor variation on the theme is incarnated in Carreen, Scarlett's sister. She is the dreamiest of the three O'Hara sisters and, as a girl of fifteen, she is in love with Brent Tarleton. Her future is prefigured early in the novel when we see her reading "a romance of a girl who had taken the veil after her lover's death." When Brent dies at Gettysburg, her life is changed forever. With the great love of her life gone, she finds solace in religion. In a weakened physical state, she contracts typhoid fever, the same disease that kills her mother, but manages to survive, and this experience only strengthens her appreciation of the hand of God in her life. Thus, hers is more and more a life of prayer. In fact, her prayer is extremely effective in saving the life of Will Benteen who wanders onto the Tara plantation as a sick man dying of pneumonia. In his agony, as he lies unconscious, Carreen sits by his bedside daily, reciting the rosary. When he finally awakens, cured, he seems to take her for the Blessed Virgin. Seeing Carreen with "the morning sun shining through her fair hair," he says to her: "Then you waren't [sic] a dream after all, I hope I ain't troubled you too much." (502) This is as close as Mitchell comes in *GWTW* to portraying a miracle, which is one of the prime ingredients of the Catholic novel, and it underlines once again the role played by the author's faith in the genesis and construction of *GWTW*.

Scarlett is irritated by Carreen's constant praying, even after she regains her health. But Will Benteen is able to understand Carreen's motivation. When Scarlett tells him that she's sick and tired of seeing Carreen do nothing but pray all day, it is he who defends her, for he realizes that she is praying for the repose of the souls of her mother and her slain beau. Unlike Scarlett, Carreen focusses her attention on the life to come after death.

At Gerald's funeral, it is also Carreen who insists that Ashley use the Catholic Book of Devotions in order to be sure that Gerald will have as Catholic a burial as possible in the absence of a priest. (698) Whether in an action like this or in days spent in prayer, she represents for Margaret Mitchell the beauty of a life devoted to union with God. Thus, when the reader finally learns that Carreen has decided to enter a convent, it is a logical outcome for her in the context of the novel. For Mitchell, this decision brings to completion her desire to pay her own personal tribute to her cousin Mattie.

Why Did Mattie Choose the Name of Melanie?

Why did Mattie select the name of Melanie when she entered religious life? After all, Melanie is not a common name for a nun and one would have to look long and hard to find another one. So where did she find this name and why did she chose it? For a first possible explanation, we look at the list of saints' canonized by the Catholic Church. According to tradition, women who entered religious life in the pre-Vatican II era would either take the name of a saint, or of a word associated with a saint of the church, like "Sister Mary Immaculata." We thus note that there are two saints named Melanie, one the granddaughter of the other and both members of an aristocratic family named the Valerii. According to church tradition, the second of the two, Melanie the Younger (c.383-438), whose feast day is on December 31, "fell in love" with and married her first cousin, Saint Pinian. They had two children who died young. Later in life they travelled to Jerusalem and decided to devote their lives to God by withdrawing from the world. Pinian entered a monastery in that city and Melanie a convent. She outlived her husband, dying in 438. Here we cannot help asking ourselves if Mattie Holliday chose the name Melanie because she had found a saint who had presumably "fallen in love" with and married her first cousin. Although we cannot be sure that she chose the name for this reason, the coincidence is striking.

A second possible explanation goes in an entirely different direction, and makes much of the combination of the name Mary with that of Melanie. Here the Melanie who might have inspired the name was the French peasant girl Melanie Mathieu-Calvat (1831-1904), the 15 year old who was one of two children (the other was an eleven year old boy named Maximin Giraud) to whom the Blessed Virgin appeared in 1846. This is the apparition at La Salette, a small village in the southeast of France near the city of Grenoble. The message, stressing the need for penance, that had been imparted to the children, was later revealed by them to Pope Pius IX in 1851 and became known in the mid-19th century as the "secret" of La Salette. It was a great wonder for the faithful in its day, although it has been overshadowed by the later apparitions at Lourdes (1858) and Fatima (1917).

After initial resistance to the story of the apparition (there was only one, not several) at La Salette, the truth of the event began to be be more widely accepted, even by the church hierarchy. Devotion to Notre Dame de la Salette was officially authorized by Rome and the huge church that had been built on the site of the apparition was elevated to the status of a basilica by Pope Leo XIII in 1879, just three years before Martha Anne Holliday entered the Sisters of Mercy. Thus, she could have selected the double name of Mary Melanie to commemorate the apparition of Mary, the Blessed Virgin, to a peasant girl named Melanie.

There remains the fact that the French peasant named Melanie was about fifteen years old at the time of this mystical revelation. This was also the age when Saint Melanie the Younger, mentioned above, married her first cousin. Significantly, this is the key age for the experience of epiphany, or revelation, in *GWTW*, for this is the age when young women like Scarlett and her mother fall in love and discover the power of their feelings. This coincidence cannot go unnoticed.

There is yet one more coincidence in this story: Melanie Mathieu-Calvat died on December 14th, which is also Mattie Holliday's birthday.

The unpublished letter that Mitchell wrote to a relative in 1947, and that has already been quoted, is helpful again here. In it, Mitchell had this to say about Mattie Holliday's selection of the name Melanie in religious life: "Her name was not Melanie - that is, by birth - it was her religious name, adopted as most sisters do at the time they leave the outside world and take up a new life and a new name." She goes on: "Melanie was a very popular name, fashionable in the days of her [Mattie Holliday's] youth. It was the name of the Countess Metternich, who made the Congress of Vienna very colorful. French refugees from Haiti brought it to Southern cities in the early 1800's and almost every family Bible shows at least one child by that name." She then goes on in a personal vein about Sister Melanie, as follows: "I am sorry you did not know her. She died fairly recently, that is, around 1944 [sic]. She loved to have her cousins call on her. She had a permanent room in St. Joseph's Infirmary, in Atlanta, not very far from my father's room. Father was in the hospital for three years prior to his death, and I frequently went to see the old lady, who dearly loved company."[24]

In summary, we cannot be sure why Martha Anne Holliday chose her religious name, although it is tempting to think that she did so because of the example of the Saint Melanie who had married her first cousin. But, as I have attempted to show in the preceding pages, the name appealed to Mitchell because it was both a widely used name in the 19th century, *and* the name that her beloved cousin had adopted in religious life. This is why and how the famous character of *GWTW* got her name.

The Catholic Idea of *contemptum mundi*

Through the juxtaposition of Scarlett on the one hand, and Ellen/Carreen on the other, Mitchell offers two competing concepts of happiness. Each one is revealed at about the age of sixteen and chosen for life by a commitment made at that time. The first and most fully developed view of happiness in *GWTW* is communicated through the experience of Scarlett, who falls in love at the age of sixteen. She remains in and of the world and is attached to all that it has to offer. But what Scarlett thinks is her love for Ashley is a mere illusion, and *GWTW* describes

---

24. As mentioned above, Mattie died in 1939. In this case, Mitchell seems to be confusing her husband's stay at St. Joseph's Infirmary in 1936-37, with that of her father between 1942 and 1944.

and analyzes the pursuit of this illusion for over a thousand pages.

With Sister Mary Melanie in mind, Mitchell created two other characters to reflect both an alternative view of happiness and her cousin's spiritual glory. The first exemplar of this type of commitment is Ellen, who marries Gerald O'Hara because she cannot have her cousin, Philippe. She would have preferred to enter a convent. But since her father would not allow it, she instead chose the married state as a way to live a life of sacrifice for others. Later, she sacrifices her own health to care for people who are considerably lower than she on the social scale. Ellen turns her back on the world and its values. In imitation of Christ, she truly lays down her life for others. Carreen continues and brings to perfection her mother's desire to enter religious life. Through this character, Mitchell brings to completion her transposition of Mattie Holliday's experience.

This image of the woman who turns her back on the world in order to live on a higher spiritual level is essential to the genesis and structure of *GWTW*, and it shows how deeply Mitchell's view of spirituality was influenced by her Catholic upbringing. The ancient Christian tradition of *contemptum mundi*, the suspicion, even hatred, of the world and its values, was an integral part of the world view that Margaret Mitchell inherited from her mother and her family.

This turning away from the world is fundamental to Mitchell's vision of life and also helps to explain her conduct once fame and celebrity suddenly entered her life in 1936. Her immediate instinct was to withdraw. She had written the novel as a private testimony to her mother, to her cousin Martha Anne Holliday, and to her family. The deluge of attention occasioned by the success of the novel disoriented her. Not only did she eschew buying a big house and making a major social splash, she also gave generously to charities in a private manner. She did everything possible to live the rest of her life in a sheltered manner out of the limelight. It can truly be said that in the last years of her life, she lived that spirit of *contemptum mundi* that she had written about so eloquently in *GWTW*.

Chapter 8:
Rhett Butler and the Confrontation with Satan

Rhett and the Garden of Earthly Delights

It is probable that Mitchell drew the inspiration for Rhett Butler from a certain number of experiences that she had had with her first husband, Berrien "Red" Kinnard Upshaw, to whom she was married from Christmas Day 1922 until the following summer. Afraid of a lawsuit from "Red" if she made Rhett physically resemble her ex-husband and, as we have seen, fanatically committed to keeping readers from being able to make any connections between characters in the novel and her private life, Mitchell completely redesigned Rhett's appearance. She wanted to make him look as different as possible from his model. Yet she did leave a clue to the origins of his identity. When Scarlett notices the initials "R.K.B." (248) on Rhett's handkerchief, no immediate explanation is offered about the meaning of the middle initial, nor is one provided elsewhere in the text of *GWTW*. Yet, as Anne Edwards has pointed out, (191) each one of the initials corresponds to one that was associated with **B**errien "**R**ed" **K**innard Upshaw.

Like "Red," Rhett is a dropout from a service academy, West Point for one and Annapolis for the other. Each is also a profiteer and a predator: just as Rhett exploits the economic blockade of the South for his own profit, "Red" ran bootleg whiskey during Prohibition. Each was also inclined to separate sex from love without much difficulty, finding it easy to put a price tag on things of the heart. But the real key to the identification between Rhett and "Red" is perhaps to be found in the chemistry, or lack of it, between each of these male figures and Scarlett/Margaret. For no matter how violent, abusive and hard drinking "Red" might have been, it still takes two to tango. The main reason why Margaret Mitchell's marriage to "Red" could not work was because their personalities were so utterly incompatible and their expectations from marriage so completely different. In a word, they had a major communication problem, and it is this aspect of Mitchell's experience that she recreates in the couple of Scarlett and Rhett. Each time that one wants to reconcile, the other does not, and each time that the lines of communication seem about to open up, a misunderstanding intervenes to close them down again.

Working with the raw materials of her lived experience, Mitchell transforms "Red" into one of the most memorable characters in American literature. In *GWTW*, Rhett Butler is the living incarnation of evil. On the surface, he is attractive and alluring, but one is well advised not to approach him too closely. One might fall under his spell. When he first appears at the barbecue at Twelve Oaks in the spring of 1861, his physical features are not presented in great detail. It is his speech that is emphasized here, and his words against the coming war make sense, especially with the advantage of hindsight. And this is precisely one of the keys to understanding the success of *GWTW*: the diabolical character who represents selfishness and egotism often makes statements about the human condition that make sense to the ordinary reader.

A year later, when Rhett appears at the dance/auction at the Armory in Atlanta, his true identity is clearly visible. Not only is he dressed in black, his body has the long silhouette of a snake, for he is "bulky in the shoulders but tapering to a small waist and absurdly small feet in varnished boots." (178-9) With "jet black hair," and a "black mustache," his massive body is "powerful and patently dangerous." In a word, he is "a man of lusty and unashamed appetites." Later, the narrative voice will tell us that he is "perverse as a demon," (668) and even goes so far as to call him a "mocking devil." (844)

In every conceivable way, Rhett is the antithesis of the more idealistic men who surround him. Rightly or wrongly, they uphold their Cause, the Confederacy, while Rhett, like Satan in rebellion against God, believes only in himself. Perhaps the clearest sign that he represents the Devil is his arrogant attitude: "he had an air of utter assurance, of displeasing insolence about him, and there was a twinkle of malice in his bold eyes." (179) When one recalls the circumstances of his second appearance at Twelve Oaks on the day of the barbecue, as the interloper in the conversation between Scarlett and Ashley in John Wilkes' library, his evil intentions come into clearer focus. As Scarlett looks up at him, she sees "two of the blackest eyes she had ever seen, dancing in merciless merriment." (179)

Later, when he comes to help Scarlett flee from Atlanta as the city is being bombarded, he "came up the walk with the springy stride of a savage and his fine head was carried like a pagan prince." (371) The danger of a city on fire affects him like an "intoxicant" and brings out his "ruthlessness." A little while later, "his dark profile stood out as clearly as the head on an ancient coin, beautiful, cruel and decadent." (377)

Like Satan, Rhett is able to see into the hearts of others and tries to bring strife wherever he can. Just looking at Scarlett he "knew she hadn't loved Charlie and he wouldn't let her pretend to the nice polite sentiments that she would express." (183) At first, Scarlett only sees him as a well-born man who is not living up to the code of his caste. By birth, he should be a "gentleman" but he doesn't behave like one. When she compares Rhett to the boys she grew up with, the Tarletons, the Calverts, and the Fontaines, she realizes that there is a major difference, "for beneath Rhett's seeming lightness there was something malicious, almost sinister in its suave brutality." (227) Yet there is something much more wrong with him than that, but she is unable to figure out what it is. Even when he "leaned down across the counter until his mouth was near her ear and hissed," (183) she still did not realize that she was dealing with Satan himself.

Another powerful proof of his satanical identity is when Scarlett, in anger with Melanie, wants to scream out "Name of God" in frustration. But when she looks at Satan in the person of Rhett Butler, all she can do is "manage a very sour smile." (186) The Devil will not allow the name of his rival to be mentioned, even when that name is taken in vain. Likewise, he is intent only on making money, no matter how much harm he does to others in the process. In fact, tearing down is no different to him from building up, for "there is just as much money to be made out of the wreckage of a civilization as from the upbuilding of one." (193) It is no accident that Rhett's father, an upright man, had "stricken his name from the family Bible." (223)

Satan is reputed to have the ability to go anywhere he wants. He is clever and wily, and is able to overcome most defenses. Is it any wonder that Rhett is such a successful blockade runner? This ability is exemplified in the way he gains entry into the home of the Hamilton family in Atlanta. During the war, Miss Pittypat wants to keep him away at all costs. Yet, once he "intended to be asked into Pittypat's house," he "knew unerringly how to get the invitation." (198)

Finally, while Christianity proposes that human relationships should be governed by the law of love, which is characterized by the willful commission of charitable acts for the benefit of others, with nothing expected in return, the law of Satan ridicules such a notion. Rhett voices this ridicule when he tells Scarlett: "Always remember I never do anything without reason and I never give anything without expecting something in return. I always get paid." (242)

Scarlett in the Devil's Clutches

Many readers of GWTW have voiced disappointment that Rhett and Scarlett separate at the end of the novel. They presumably react this way because they see the two protagonists as being very much alike, and therefore well suited to each other. But nothing could be further from the truth, for Rhett is not the right person for Scarlett - or any other woman, for that matter.

GWTW is a cautionary tale about love and money, self-understanding and illusion, domination and subjection. When Scarlett falls under the spell of Rhett, her already flabby moral life gets even flabbier. She gouges her workers even more than she had before, lives arrogantly in a tasteless and ostentatious house, and does not even concern herself with the basics, like seeing that her son Wade attends church on Sunday. Ironically, it is Rhett who has to do this, just to keep up appearances, for even the Devil knows the importance of appearances.

By the end of GWTW Scarlett has reached a moral dead end. She is no longer a Catholic, and does not even respect the Catholic ideals inculcated in her as a child. In this, she is quite different from Mitchell herself who, by the time she began writing her novel around 1926 might not have been a weekly churchgoer, but still had a tremendous respect for Catholicism, as her novel amply demonstrates. Thus, *GWTW* tries to show the danger of seeking only earthly rewards, with no consideration for the spiritual dimension in this life, or the reality of an afterlife.

In this weakened spiritual state, there is very little likelihood that Scarlett will ever be able to save her soul if she reunites with Rhett. Conversely, after his departure, her chances for earning her salvation improve accordingly. Thus, the solitude in which we find Scarlett at the end of *GWTW* is a positive development in her life, for it is only in this situation that she will begin to ponder the most important questions in life, get her moral priorities in order, and reform her life before it is too late.

Chapter 9:
Prayer and the Catholic
Examination of Conscience

Ellen's Religious Impact on her Daughter

The character of Ellen Robillard O'Hara plays a dual role in *GWTW*. She evokes the McGhan ancestry, while also representing several aspects of the life of May Belle Mitchell. These matters were treated in Chapter 3. But this dimension of her character, i. e., the Scarlett/ Ellen relationship, also allows Mitchell to explore further the role that religion played in her own relationship with her mother.

Ellen has a mesmerizing effect on her oldest daughter, Scarlett. Raising her as a devout Catholic, she has inculcated in the young girl the cult of the Blessed Virgin. Margaret Mitchell no doubt penned these pages with ease, and culled them from the massive blocks of her childhood memories of her mother. In *GWTW*, Scarlett is so impressed by both the power of the message itself, that is, the example of availability and service to others as found in what we know of the life of the Blessed Virgin, and by the person who conveyed it, Ellen, that as a child she conflates the two and considers her mother "as something holy and apart from the rest of humankind." When she watches her mother leading the family in the recitation of the rosary, it is as if her mother were in fact a re-incarnation herself of the Blessed Virgin. "As always since childhood, this was, for Scarlett, a moment of adoration of Ellen, rather than the Virgin. Sacrilegious though it might be, Scarlett always saw, through her closed eyes, the upturned face of Ellen and not the Blessed Virgin, as the ancient phrases were repeated. "Health of the Sick," "Seat of Wisdom," "Refuge of Sinners," "Mystical Rose," - they were beautiful because they were the attributes of Ellen." (73)

Margaret Mitchell had been raised as a Catholic. She was baptized, confirmed, and made her First Communion at Sacred

Heart Parish. This was her spiritual home as a child. May Belle had been baptized by the legendary Fr. O'Reilly of Immaculate Conception Parish in the center of the city. When the new Sacred Heart Parish was carved out of it, the Stephenses were numbered among the founding members. Socially speaking, they were also among the half dozen or so most prominent families of the new parish. The rites and rituals of pre-Vatican II Catholicism were a part and parcel of Margaret's life as a child. And since the seeds of any great novel are sown in the writer's childhood, which contains her most sensitive years, it was inevitable that Catholicism should play a major role in *GWTW*. In fact, I would go so far as to say that an appreciation of the Catholic element in the novel is essential for a full understanding of its meaning.

Margaret Mitchell progressively wandered away from Catholicism as an adolescent, and abandoned active practice of her faith while she was in college. After May Belle's death, this rejection of the externals of Catholicism caused a strain in relations with her grandmother, Annie Fitzgerald Stephens. If she felt that she had, in a sense, made a pact with the Devil in deciding to no longer be a practicing Catholic, she never took up the practice of any other religion in its place. But by this time, as she began to write in 1926, May Belle was no longer on the scene. And what would she think about her daughter's laxity in matters religious? Would she approve? Scarlett's (and Margaret's) anxiety about this is reflected any number of times in the novel. In fact, to the degree that Scarlett thinks first about her own welfare and only belatedly of that of others, a tactic that permits her to indulge her two obsessions (marrying Ashley and holding onto the deed to Tara), she is unfaithful to her mother's teachings, which emphasize concern for others. In the second half of *GWTW*, this becomes a major theme, which can be labelled "what would your mother think?" (654) Each time that this question arises, the authorial voice seems to express a longing for a return to the original, privileged situation before the distractions of adulthood separated the two women.

As an example of this, as noted in Chapter 6, Scarlett's conscience rebels when she says the word "nigger," (394), which was specifically forbidden by her mother. These stirrings of conscience are linked to her steady moral decline, which begins in earnest after her return to Tara. We see it clearly, for instance, after she kills the Yankee soldier who intrudes into the house at Tara. When she removes the wallet from his pocket and sees all the money in it, she stares at the bills and tells herself that there is a God after all. (436) Money now becomes her obsession in life

Later, when she tells herself that a woman cannot be a lady without money, her conscience rebels once again, for she knows that Ellen would disagree with such an idea. Those women of her class who are now destitute still consider themselves to be ladies despite their poverty, and Scarlett tries to convince herself that they are fools. But then, in a "flash of revelation, she realized vaguely that, foolish though they seemed, theirs was the right attitude. Ellen would have thought so. This disturbed her. She knew she should feel as these people felt, but she could not. She knew she should believe devoutly, as they did, that a born lady remained a lady, even if reduced to poverty, but she could not make herself believe it now." She continues, "It took money to be a lady. She knew Ellen would have fainted had she ever heard such words from her daughter." (600)

Driven by her obsession, "she strained forward feverishly in her pursuit of money and still more money." (652) She is willing to lie and steal in order to increase her wealth, but her conscience, in the thought of what her mother would say to all this, pursues her. "The first time Scarlett lied in this fashion, she felt disconcerted and guilty - disconcerted because the lie sprang so easily and naturally from her lips, guilty because the thought flashed in her mind: What would Mother say? There was no doubt what Ellen would say to a daughter who told lies and engaged in sharp practices. She would be stunned and incredulous and would speak gentle words that stung despite their gentleness, would talk of honor, honesty and truth and duty to one's neighbor." (654) But by now Scarlett is tired of feeling guilty, and hereafter concludes that she'll think about questions of conscience tomorrow: "I'll think of all this later." (654)

Thus, by the end of the novel, when Scarlett has sacrificed everything for money, she still clings to the memory of her mother. Just like the little girl who said repeatedly to her mother: "I'm always your little girl," (218) she repeats the same formula as an adult. In a moment of lucidity, she confides to Rhett, for example: "No one ever really liked me, except Mother."

(672) Finally, at the end of the novel, she realizes the connection between Ellen and Melanie, both of whom loved her unconditionally: "Melly is the only woman friend I ever had, the only woman except Mother who really loved me. She's like Mother, too." (1000)

Among other things, *GWTW* is the story of a young woman's progressive discovery of the world; and in the case of Scarlett it involves the gradual wandering away from the moral foundation given to her by her mother. As we have seen, Scarlett's conscience reminds her, and Mammy says to her out loud, that her mother would never approve of some particular action, or would be turning over in her grave if she knew about it. It is only when Scarlett realizes that she herself no longer believes in prayer, that she becomes more conscious of her mother's - and Carreen's - regular devotion to it. "Carreen . . . prayed a good deal, for when Scarlett came into her room without knocking, she always found her on her knees by her bed. The sight never failed to annoy her, for Scarlett felt that the time for prayer had passed. If God had seen fit to punish them so, then God could very well do without prayers. Religion had always been a bargaining process with Scarlett. She promised God good behavior in exchange for favors. God had broken the bargain time and time again, to her way of thinking, and she felt that she owed Him nothing at all now." (502)

A passage like this reflects convictions that were deeply held by Margaret Mitchell for the first few years after her return to Atlanta as a young adult. By the time she wrote *GWTW*, she had informally broken with the Church and no longer actively practiced her faith. Like Scarlett in her early twenties, she seems to have even become downright hostile to the faith of her childhood. And this feeling of estrangement was complicated by personality conflicts within her family. Anne Edwards tells us that May Belle's "funeral was a distressing affair. Some of the Stephens family having been so incensed at the disregard Margaret and Stephens paid to 'proper Catholic rites' that they stalked out of the cemetery before the eulogy was spoken." (59)

After her mother's death in January 1919, Margaret returned to Smith and finished out the school year. But instead of returning to Northampton in the following fall, she remained in the family nest at 1401 Peachtree Street with her father, brother and grandmother. Since, according to Edwards, she "had left the church for good following the angry scene at her mother's funeral," she felt very uncomfortable living with her pious grandmother. Annie Fitzgerald Stephens's "enforced evening prayers had been a great source of conflict when she had come to stay at Peachtree Street. Getting down on her knees in her own home was something Peggy Mitchell simply could not and would not do." (72) This feeling is reflected in the revulsion that Scarlett feels when she sees Carreen - an extension of Ellen - praying. Thus, it was only a question of time until she asked her grandmother to move out, which only strained relations even further with the Irish and Catholic side of her family. Margaret might act like a "modern woman," but in doing so she cut a few critical family bridges behind her. She would henceforth be estranged from the Fitzgerald/Stephens side of her family - except, of course, for Sister Mary Melanie, who always loved her, just as Melanie always loved Scarlett.

Ironically, as *GWTW* makes clear, this apparent break with the Church and with the Catholic side of her family did not erase them from her life. Whether or not Mitchell actually ceased to believe is a matter of conjecture. On the other hand, it is certain that after this break she became more and more aware of the debt that she owed to her mother and to her Irish forebears. In fact, I would go so far as to say that one of her main goals when she set about writing *GWTW* was to attempt to delineate for posterity her understanding and appreciation of that debt.

Prayer in *GWTW*

Prayer, which can be defined as the lifting of the mind and heart to God, recurs throughout *GWTW*. Both Ellen and Scarlett pray, although each does so in a different manner. This theme illustrates the continuity between mother and daughter, while also emphasizing the major difference between them.

Mitchell uses the theme of prayer to probe some of the differences in world view between herself and her mother. For instance, prayer is difficult for Scarlett, since "religion went no more than lip deep with her." (71) Nonetheless, the thought of her mother kneeling in prayer was precious: "It was not the lifting up of her heart to God that brought this balm...[but] the sight of her mother's serene face upturned to the throne of God and His saints and angels, praying for blessings on those whom she loved." (71) Maybelle Stephens Mitchell's memory is perpetuated for all time in this cameo portrait by her daughter.

Prayer is so important in *GWTW* that it it can be used as one of several possible structuring devices to understand the work's development. Scarlett prays, however fitfully, selfishly and unsuccessfully, throughout the first half of *GWTW*. To the extent that she is essentially wild and relatively uncivilized, like her father, she is not naturally inclined to pray. In fact, the only prayers that Gerald knows are the few phrases of Latin that he had memorized when he was an altar boy in Ireland in his youth - and Scarlett is like him. She has "the easily stirred passions of her Irish father," and "nothing except the thinnest veneer of her mother's unselfish and forbearing nature." Or again, "she had Gerald's Irish temper along with the deceptive sweetness of face she had inherited from Ellen." (218) Throughout the first half of the novel, her personality is compared to that of her father, while she clearly has her mother's looks. Then, abruptly, when she realizes that God will not deliver Ashley into her hands, she stops praying for good. "When such thoughts came she did not pray hastily to God, telling Him she did not mean it. God did not frighten her any more." (499) But when Scarlett stops praying, she loses any comfort or guidance that it affords. The graces that Catholic theology teaches come to anyone who prays, no matter how imperfectly, cease to flow in her direction.

From here on, she strays further and further from her mother's teachings, and as she does so, she begins to look more and more like her father. Mammy, her figurative guardian angel, is the first to notice the change. "Lordy, 'twas right funny how de older Miss Scarlett git de mo' she look lak Mist' Gerald and de less lak Miss Ellen!" (536) She seems to want to imitate her father's immigrant experience, and in so doing put the model of her mother's behavior and standards out of sight: "She was going to rush into life and wrest from it what she could. Her father had started as a poor immigrant boy and had won the broad acres of Tara. What he had done, his daughter could do." (601) After all, she is her father's daughter, and "Gerald's blood was in her, violent blood." (640) Scarlett's progressive loss of contact with mother and the pious values and practices that she represents, is symbolized in Bonnie, Scarlett's child by Rhett. To the extent that the child is the living reincarnation of Gerald, and owes nothing to Ellen, she shows how Scarlett has strayed from all that her mother stood for. The daughter is remarkable for "her complete resemblance to Gerald O'Hara." (963) And just before the little girl's death in a jumping accident, which repeats Gerald's experience, Scarlett realizes that Bonnie's eyes "are like Pa's eyes. Irish blue eyes and she's like him in every way." (979)

The Catholic Examination of Conscience

The examination of conscience (335) was one of the fundamental spiritual practices in pre-Vatican II spirituality. It was both a form of prayer and a prelude to prayer. Mitchell explores this question a number of times in *GWTW*, for it is critical both to the development of Scarlett as a character and to the exorcising of her own personal demons in writing the book. For Scarlett, who tends to always seek her own interest and advantage, the examination of conscience serves as an occasional call to order in her life.

Here is an example of how Mitchell uses this theme. When Scarlett realizes that she loves a man who is determined to marry someone else, "she knew she should be examining her conscience. Ellen had taught her that at the end of each day it was her duty to examine her conscience, to admit her numerous faults and pray to God for forgiveness and strength never to repeat them. But Scarlett was examining her heart." (72)

This question arises again when Scarlett ponders her action as she secretly reads Ashley's letters to Melanie. She wonders what her mother would say if she knew of such behavior, (208) but then dismisses the thought. Here she is already distancing herself from her strict Catholic upbringing in what might seem like a little thing. But before long, this little thing will lead to much bigger things. Thanks no doubt to her own personal experience, Mitchell skillfully paints this portrait of the moral slide away from the mother's rules toward laxity. "When Scarlett first began reading these letters she had been so stricken of conscience and so fearful of discovery she could hardly open the envelopes for trembling. Now, her never too scrupulous sense of honor was dulled by repetition of the offense and even fear of discovery had subsided." But still she cannot help but ask herself: "What would Mother say if she knew?" (208) It is here for the first time in *GWTW* that the theme of deferment of moral judgment is introduced when Scarlett tells herself: "I'll think about it tomorrow," (208) rather than dealing with the problem right away.

To be sure, one of Scarlett's most difficult problems with prayer is knowing what to pray for. Unfortunately, it usually includes being granted some favor that will allow her to draw close to Ashley. For not only does she think of him while her family is reciting the rosary, she also prays to be alone with him when he returns to Atlanta on furlough at Christmas time 1863. Later, when she learns that he has been captured and imprisoned, she reaches for her rosary and attempts to offer a prayer for his safety. Now her loss of faith appears to her in its grim reality: "Once in the house, Scarlett stumbled up the stairs to her bedroom and, clutching her Rosary from the table, dropped to her knees and tried to pray. But the prayers would not come. There only fell on her an abysmal fear, a certain knowledge that God had turned His face from her for her sin. She had loved a married man and tried to take him from his wife, and God had punished her by killing him." (280) Ever more self-centered, she can only see reality from a selfish point of view. At one point, she even goes so far as to pray to the Blessed Virgin: "Mary, Mother of God, let me think of a real good lie." (586)

By the time she marries Rhett, she no longer prays or even attends church. The moral teachings that her mother had attempted to impart to her have been lost. Even Rhett notices what has happened to her conscience: "No, I don't love you. But I do like you tremendously - for the elasticity of your conscience, [and] for the selfishness which you seldom trouble to hide. . ." (335) Thus, it should come as no surprise to us that by the end of the novel, Scarlett has "no religion left." (1013)

Chapter 10:
The Rosary and Other Pious Practices

The Rosary as a Family Experience

The rosary is probably the essential form of Catholic prayer in *GWTW*. As a form of prayer, it has always had the advantage that any fixed and ritualized prayer has over one that is more personal and introspective. It is not easy to pray, as anyone who has tried knows, and the rosary, by providing words and a focus, is meant to make it easier to to so. (340, 502, 701)

This pious practice originated with Saint Dominic (1170-1221) in twelfth century Italy. It gained popularity very rapidly and has been the most widespread Marian devotion among Catholics for the last 700 years. The rosary consists of the recitation of a series of set prayers divided into five decades. These five decades are in turn devoted the to joyous, sorrowful and glorious mysteries of Mary's life. Thus, a complete Rosary would consist of fifteen decades.

Each decade consists of "the Lord's Prayer," said once, followed by "the Hail Mary," which is recited ten times. This prayer is inspired by the words of the angel Gabriel to Mary as recorded in Luke I, 28. Its words are: "Hail Mary, full of grace, the Lord is with Thee. Blessed art thou among women and blessed is the fruit of thy womb, Jesus. Holy Mary, Mother of God, pray for us sinners, now and at the hour of our death. Amen." Each decade is ended by the brief prayer "Glory be to the Father, and to the Son, and to the Holy Spirit."

In *GWTW*, the O'Hara family says a rosary of five decades. Although Scarlett's attention wavers half way through as she turns her mind to her world of illusion, which is governed by the vision of Ashley, she is able to refocus on the rosary before the evening prayers are over. Mitchell recounts for the reader what must have been her own experience of the healing power of prayer in this way: "The kneeling figures, the soft glow of the lamp, the dim shadows where the negroes swayed, even the familiar objects that had been so hateful to her sight an hour ago, in an instant took on the color of her own emotions, and the room seemed once more a lovely place. She would never forget this moment or this scene!" (73) Despite Mitchell's break with her grandmother, Annie Fitzgerald Stephens, which was caused in part by the latter's insistence on formal evening prayers at 1401 Peachtree Street, she still bears witness to the beauty of prayer in a united family.

At the beginning of *GWTW*, the rosary is Scarlett's preferred form of prayer. It is from her mother that she has learned to pray the rosary, as seen in one of the opening scenes of the novel, in which the whole family recites the rosary after dinner. Later, when Gerald sends a letter to Atlanta informing Scarlett that her sister Carreen has typhoid fever, he adds that "Mrs. O'Hara said Scarlett must go to church and say some Rosaries for Carreen's recovery." (329) Finally, when she learns that her mother and sister are sick with typhoid fever, she immediately falls on her knees and murmurs what is probably her most sincere prayer of the novel. "No formal Rosaries now but the same words over and over: "Mother of God, don't let her die! I'll be so good if you don't let her die! Please, don't let her die!'" (340)

Closely related to the rosary is the Litany of the Blessed Virgin. It is recited at the conclusion of the family rosary early in *GWTW*. (173) The litany originated in the earliest centuries of the Christian era and reflects the continuous reverence that Christians have had since earliest times for Mary, the Mother of Jesus. There are 49 salutations contained in the complete Litany of the Blessed Virgin. Each salutation is read by one person, to which all others in attendance respond: "Pray for us." In *GWTW*, Mitchell includes five of the forty-nine salutations: "Virgin Most Faithful," "Health of the Sick," "Seat of Wisdom," "Refuge of Sinners," and "Mystical Rose." There are also several instances later in the novel in which references are made to the Litany, usually in the oft-repeated expletive "Mother of God," which resonates from one end of *GWTW* to the other

The Power of the Rosary

Soon after Scarlett decides that she will no longer pray, two important things happen that are linked specifically to the rosary. First, Will Benteen almost dies from pneumonia but as we have seen, Carreen's prayer vigil at his bedside seems to save him. When he recovers his senses, he sees her sitting there, "telling her rosary beads." (502) He then says: "Then you warn't a dream, after all. I hope I ain't troubled you too much M'am." It is as if, in his delirium, he had seen her interceding for him. Here, the authorial voice of *GWTW* posits prayer as an effective antidote to suffering, going so far as to even suggest miraculous powers in this instance. But on the same page Scarlett comes into Carreen's room at Tara and finds her on her knees praying. She is annoyed at this, seeing no connection between her sister's prayers and Will's recovery. Scarlett is angry about what the war has done to them all, and she holds God guilty: ". . .if God had seen fit to punish them so, then God could very well do without prayers." (502) Anecdotal reference to the rosary is also made several times. For instance, when Charles Hamilton is about to embark for Virginia, he asks Scarlett if she will pray for him while he is away. To mollify the boy, she promises to say "three Rosaries a night, at least." Likewise, when she is in despair at the barbecue because Ashley is going to marry Melanie, she retreats to the library at Twelve Oaks where she begins praying: "Hail Mary, full of grace," (117) the basic prayer of the rosary.

Despite the importance of the rosary to Scarlett, reference is also made to other, less formal prayers, that are said on the spur of the moment. One example of the many instances of such prayers in *GWTW* is when Scarlett sees John Wilkes riding off to defend Atlanta with the Home Guard. Afraid that he might not return, he tells her that he would have liked to see his grandchild. "Then in superstitious terror she crossed herself and tried to say a prayer," (310) and this time, she succeeds, praying that both Ashley and his father will be safe.

Catholic Prayers for the Dead

The scene in which Gerald O'Hara is buried (701) is surely linked to Mitchell's experience of her mother's death and burial. Here, because the Catholic side of her family felt that the graveside services were too Protestant and not sufficiently Catholic, they walked off before the completion of the eulogy. Mitchell was hurt by this, and bridges between her and them were seriously cut at this time. Knowing of this experience, the reader can better appreciate the way she paints the scene.

Here it is Scarlett's sister, Carreen, who will later become a Sister of Mercy, who plays the role of the traditional Catholic. In the absence of a priest, she has decided to employ the Book of Devotions that was in use at the time and which was specifically designed for such occasions. Catholics who lived in an area where there were no or very few priests still had to conduct Catholic baptisms and burials, and this book helped them to do it.

In her depiction of this scene, Mitchell stresses Scarlett's reactions. First, she is happy that Ashley is reading the prayers from the Book of Devotions and that a priest is not present, because the latter would be a stranger. Next, when Ashley omits the prayers about purgatory, she is pleased that he has done so, because the local country folk had probably never heard of purgatory and would be miffed to think that anyone would assume that a good neighbor and a loyal Confederate like Gerald O'Hara could have gone anywhere but straight to heaven. Next comes the time for a common prayer.

> The gathering joined heartily in the Lord's Prayer but their voices trailed off into embarrassed silence when he began the Hail Mary. They had never heard that prayer and they looked furtively at each other as the O'Hara girls, Melanie and the Tara servants gave the response; 'Pray for us, now and at the hour of our death. Amen.'"

At this point the Catholic burial service is over. The Catholic fixed prayers are at an end, and Carreen, the emblem of the traditional Catholic, expects Ashley to make this clear. But Ashley also knows that these people are now expecting a eulogy "as they settled themselves in easier positions for a long harangue." (701) What to do? Ashley, because of his familiarity with the middle ground of the Episcopal burial service, strikes a compromise between the Catholic and Baptist modes of prayer. He recites a few more prayers from memory, and then asks the attendees if they would like to eulogize Gerald.

The scene unmistakably expresses Mitchell's ambivalence

about the Catholic Church and its rigid ceremonial code. She admires its beauty, but implicitly condemns its lack of flexibility. Here, as the authorial voice preaches understanding, acceptance and reconciliation between denominations, Mitchell herself seems to be striving to smooth out the rough edges of her experience at her mother's burial.

But this is precisely why she wrote the novel in the first place. So many things had been left unsaid between her and her mother during the latter's lifetime, and then, after May Belle's death, even her funeral was a new cause for family strife. But in writing *GWTW*, Margaret was able, as we have seen, to transform many of these experiences. Through art, she was able to rewrite the crooked lines of her past and make them straight, and in the process achieve and complete the long-deferred union with her mother.

Conclusion

There are many prisms through which to look at *GWTW*, and until now no one has used this particular one to shed light on the novel. It is hoped that this essay will help readers to understand better a crucial aspect of the novel, one that I believe even Mitchell herself had lost sight of when she took the novel up again in 1935 and prepared it for publication. Written in a wave of creative fury between 1926 and 1928, the novel's original inspiration had passed. By 1935, she had stuffed it in drawers and paper bags all over her apartment and had pretty much forgotten it. So when the book became successful and critics began to discuss it, it was described as being completely "Southern," with no ethnic or sectarian dimensions to it. The many Catholic elements were almost completely overlooked. This state of affairs prevailed throughout Mitchell's lifetime, and she never bothered to offer corrections or clarifications. And so, gradually, contact was lost with the novel's critical Irish and Catholic roots.

Since this essay is an attempt to take a new and fresh look at Margaret Mitchell's great novel in the light of her Irish and Catholic family origins, the question will arise for some readers: am I claiming that *GWTW* is a "Catholic novel?"

The answer is both "yes" and "no," depending on how we define the term "Catholic novel." If by that expression we refer to the total ambiance of the work, the answer must be negative. After all, the Catholic threads uncovered and analyzed herein represent only a part, albeit an important one, of a large and complicated tapestry. The scope of the novel is truly vast and the Catholic thread, though important, is still not constantly visible to the reader.

But if we consider the "Catholic novel" as one in which the author poses the question of the journey of a pilgrim soul through life, and then specifically incorporates elements from the Catholic world view to bolster, support and comment upon that journey, including references to the sacraments, Catholic prayers and pious practices, and the Catholic theological interpretation of the role of grace, then we have to answer in the affirmative. In addition, Mitchell also includes both a character who shares many characteristics with Satan, and a miracle scene, the one in which Will Benteen seems to be cured through the prayers of Carreen O'Hara. All these elements justify calling the work, albeit with reservations, a "Catholic novel."

In conclusion, here is an anecdotal story handed down by word of mouth among priests who have served at Sacred Heart Church in Atlanta, where Margaret Mitchell was baptized and confirmed. According to this story, which Mitchell's biographers have refrained from telling, as she lay at death's door after her horrible automobile accident in 1949, she received the sacrament of Extreme Unction, the so-called "last sacrament" of the Church, which prepared her soul for its departure into eternal life.

So the Lord did not forget her in her hour of need. A fitting reward indeed for a dutiful soul who had given so much to others.

Index